WHAT PEOPLE ARE SAYING ABOUT

CAPITALISED EDUCATION

Kate Middleton is an international celebrity, as well as a crucial figure in the biological, economic, and cultural reproduction of the British class system. In this book, David R Cole offers us a multifaceted analysis of Middleton as "media object." Touching on topics as diverse as courtly love in medieval Europe and derivatives markets in contemporary finance, Capitalised Education traces a web of far-flung relationships that fatally lead us back to the absurdities of our collective fascination with the British Royal Family.
Steven Shaviro, Wayne State University

The pomp and ceremony of a royal wedding might seem a strange anachronism in a world of global finance and cyber-capitalism. Yet, as David Cole demonstrates, the two are folded intricately into each other. Through an immanent materialist analysis that brings together key recent and historical moments or 'plateaus' in the emergence of capitalism, liberalism, and constitutional monarchy, and culminating in Kate Middleton's 2011 marriage to Prince William, Cole's wide ranging and provocative work reveals the complex and subtle ways in which capitalism's decoding and deterritorialization go hand-in-hand with the continuation of social privileges and hierarchies. Along the way he speaks to the m   the last century (liberalism, cor   nd decolonization), the globaliza   ial crisis, and more. Linking thes   ing theories of radical political acuon, Cole traces the moments of rupture that might allow another politics to come to the fore.
Nathan Widder, Royal Holloway, University of London

Cole has produced a masterful and critical evaluation of how the British Monarchy continues to assert and grow its influence in the 21st century. He significantly contributes to an almost muted discourse which critically explores how this influence is achieved and what is risked and gained in its attainment. The reader can't but be left with a desire to question whether we should be comfortable with the process and effects this has on our behaviour, development and socialisation.

Roberto H Parada, University of Western Sydney

Capitalised Education

An immanent materialist account
of Kate Middleton

Capitalised Education

An immanent materialist account
of Kate Middleton

David R. Cole

Winchester, UK
Washington, USA

First published by Zero Books, 2014
Zero Books is an imprint of John Hunt Publishing Ltd., Laurel House, Station Approach,
Alresford, Hants, SO24 9JH, UK
office1@jhpbooks.net
www.johnhuntpublishing.com
www.zero-books.net

For distributor details and how to order please visit the 'Ordering' section on our website.

Text copyright: David R. Cole 2013

ISBN: 978 1 78279 036 5

A CIP catalogue record for this book is available from the British Library.

Design: Stuart Davies

Printed in the USA by Edwards Brothers Malloy

We operate a distinctive and ethical publishing philosophy in all
areas of our business, from our global network of authors to
production and worldwide distribution.

CONTENTS

Introduction to 'Capitalised Education'

An immanent materialist account of Kate Middleton

The Hindus teach that the Heaven World is more dangerous for the soul than the Hell World, since it is more deceptive and conduces to the fatal error of overconfidence and assumption of immunity. Like a fighter, the soul must be constantly in training lest it grow soft on an ephemeral throne. So the splendour of the palace, the constant parades, the state barges, the gold and lapis lazuli, the chariots and bowmen, eat away one's awareness of the ultimate reality of conflict.[1]

On April the 29th, 2011, I attended a performance of an amateur stage show which included my nine-year-old daughter as a backing dancer and singer in the western Sydney suburb of Penrith, Australia. This was the day of the royal wedding in London, UK, and as I sat in the third row of the audience, I noticed that many people in the hall were dressed as fake princes, princesses, kings and queens. I wondered: Were the people of Penrith making an ironic and rather silly gesture? Or were they actually saluting the royal event respectfully from across the globe, but in this peculiar and 'clownish' way? Later that night, as I watched the events of the royal wedding unfold on my Chinese made, flat-screen television, with commentary by the celebrity persona Dame Edna Everage, and with an almost exclusive focus on the apparel of the wedding guests, I realised something more fundamental and alarming about the truth of what was taking place. That realisation led me to write these words, and forces the research necessary to square the almost unfathomable conundrum that was presented by the processes and reality of the royal wedding on April the 29th, 2011. I want to express these paradoxes and charades in straightforward terms and in direct statements, yet of course, I cannot, because the sequence of events that has produced April the 29th, 2011, are far more involved, historical, affective and complex than any simple rendition or description can evoke. Rather, one requires a philosophical analysis, and a book length treatment of the strange and oddly recurrent happenings of that day, with a sustained and penetrating focus on the creation of the central character. This character is not a heroine in a romance novel, nor is she a result of breeding, nor wholly of her specific 'capitalised education', though this term does go some way to explain how Kate Middleton came to be exactly where she was on the day of the wedding. The capitalised education of this book's title refers to the ways in which the factors analysed and revealed by this book's plateaux come together and produce palpable social and cultural effects through Kate Middleton as media object. Kate is not defined by the term 'capitalised education', but it does act as a connective plane through which the complicated factors in her production (chapters 1-6) can be understood. This book deals with Kate Middleton through the philosophical lens of 'immanent materialism'[2]. Immanent materialism is a term that explains the production of plateaux such as that of April the 29th, 2011, and the proper name 'Kate Middleton' as the locus of this specific plateau (chapter 7). This book describes a weird knot of bio-cultural accidents that have conjoined the movement of post-modern capital with: social-climbing, heterosexuality, Christian union, elite education, female body-image, clothes sales and the maintenance of royal privilege.

It should be clear to the reader that I am not using the proper name of Kate Middleton in a recognisably human or ascribed manner. Her biography is only of interest in that it demonstrates aspects of the 'plateau' of April the 29th, 2011 (see chapter 7 for specific detail about Kate's biography), as a background to a 'capitalised education', and to suggest how Kate Middleton as an object now has a secret, mesmerising life of its own, beyond any direct human or societal control — as a potent media 'strange attractor' in capital space. I am not at all interested in Kate Middleton the person, but rather the focus here is on the web of synchronisations, power games and lies that conflated the presentation of the British royal family with the manipulation of the global media on the day of the royal wedding in 2011, as a means to (re)present power and within this (re)presentation to posit 'themselves' as immovable, timeless objects, worthy and capable of maintaining their positions. Immanent materialism is in many ways a demanding intellectual position to take on the production of Kate Middleton, as it requires an examination of the non-linear history that makes up the royal wedding and which foregrounds the plateau of April the 29th, 2011. In contrast to historical or dialectical materialism, which might assume a linear, class-based set of historical events that explains how the British royal family now uses and exploits the media to maintain its power to the disadvantage of those below its remit, immanent materialism examines the chaotic material processes that have gone to produce Kate Middleton in an affective, vitalist and non-linear fashion. The point here is not that the production of Kate Middleton as media object has happened spontaneously or mystically, but that the processes that have produced and are producing Kate Middleton are now weaving a strange web around us as consumers of the continuing existence of the British royal family. We are now 'subjectivised' as media watchers, and as participants in a particular phase of capitalism. In this phase, one's media image is uppermost, as it positions one in the global media market, and this image must have an impact to sell products. The market will register that something has happened for the media image to be deemed successful (i.e. sales) — market fluctuation is therefore essential, and these changes will be calcu-lated through the numbers of magazines or clothes sales regis-tered in the cash tills of high street shops, or in the tendencies in the prices of commodities attached to these products. The people in Penrith, deciding upon, going out and buying or making their

fake royal costumes to parade in the auditorium, were participating in a global phenomenon: this is an international, one
world system, whereby we are connected in previously unreal-
isable and hyper-commercial ways. The people of Penrith's
subjective inclinations, or my bemused reaction to such 'fancy
dress', are irrelevant compared to the ways in which Kate
Middleton as media object now directs global trade and its
requisite attitudes.

The chapters of this book will bring us to the point of understanding Kate Middleton as the media focus that she is today
through an examination of plateaux that have defined the ways
in which the British royal family have negotiated the power
struggles around them. I borrow the term 'plateau' from Deleuze
and Guattari's (1988) usage in *1000 Plateaus*, who in turn took the
term from Gregory Bateson's understanding of social-biological-
cultural power, and its webs of interconnected subsidiary
phenomena[3]. The point here is not to merely look for ways in
which Kate Middleton coheres as a focal media point of
commercial and societal interest, but to adjust to the perception
that behind and throughout the production of Kate Middleton as
object lies an often hidden, defamiliarised, and murky history of
cultural-political-biological intrigue and manipulation. My
position in this book of immanent materialism is parallel and
complementary to recent developments in speculative realism
that have looked to apply and develop themes in philosophical
inquiry around ideas of the inhuman, unhuman, post-human,
non-human and thinking which has not been over-extended,
adulterated and saturated by human modes of thought, i.e.,
normalisation and over-coding. However, I will stay with
immanent materialism as the philosophical position of this book
derived from Deleuze and Guattari (1988) primarily for two
reasons amidst the current renaissance in open access publishing
and hyperlinked blogging of speculative realism, non-
philosophy and the many shades of multi-vitalism[4]:

4

1. Immanent materialism is explicitly political. Many commentators have spoken about the ways in which one should read Deleuze and Guattari (1988) or otherwise, yet the fact remains that their work still has political valence and application, in this case to look at the production of Kate Middleton as media object and a capitalised education. The materialist aspect of the thesis requires that we rigorously question the ways in which capital has flowed and money has been manipulated throughout history to end up with the object of Kate Middleton that we are left with in contemporary culture. Embedded with this rigorous and explicit questioning of the modes of becoming of the British royal family, is the ontological fact that at each juncture and crossing point where the capital flows may be recognisably ascribed, are the ways in which subjectification and subjection to particular regimes of control have been immanent. Thus a type of political layering is produced that works on many levels and needs to be peeled away before one realises the real effects of Kate Middleton as media object in contemporary culture. The politics of immanent materialism is under-girthed by the philosophical and scientific positions of Spinoza, Bergson, Nietzsche, Marx, and ethological work as a development of Darwinian evolution, e.g. in the terms of Jakob von Uexküll such as the *umwelt*[5].

2. Immanent materialism is in this book an example of applied philosophy. Whilst I believe that the construction of the position of immanent materialism is rigorous and fully locatable in the history of philosophy, I do not wish to dwell on the specific metaphysical system that has derived immanent materialism as such. The primary locus of this study is Kate Middleton as media convergence and object. The secondary objects in this study are the focal points and control mechanisms of post-industrial capitalism that maintain Kate Middleton (henceforth sometimes referred to

as KM) as object and the subjective positioning that is ascribed to KM as object. One of the most relevant ways in which this happens is through learning. We now learn about KM as media object, and are saturated with this (re)constituted thought by existing and negotiating in contemporary culture. As such, the use of immanent materialism introduces 'learning' as a vital means to understand how our brains are now structured and (re)structured to recognise KM as media object and to behave accordingly. For example, the people in Australia of Penrith dress up in fake costumes, wedding guests trot along happily to the wedding with their partners and in their 'Sunday best', and I react with a certain amount of revulsion and credulity at the unremitting, naked power displayed on my flat-screen TV on the other side of the world. These behaviours have come about due to learning, and immanent materialism introduces the many-layered thought of learning about the media focus of KM as a historical and affective presence. The future of KM is involved and mixed up with these thoughts, yet this future is defined as a bio-cultural knot of tendencies and flows, that may alter as the ways in which the British royal family incur capital differentiation (currently increasing) and the world economic environment changes. This study therefore has a parallel and complementary underbelly in learning and education to explain KM as a sustained media object which is through the unconscious constructivism of immanent materialism.

In his early work called *Virtual Geography*, McKenzie Wark[6] speaks about 'events' in terms of multi-dimensional and paradoxical situations wherein media coverage reveals something profound about the audience, society and historical framing of what is broadcast through the media. The event that Wark concentrated on was the one where Saddam Hussein was shown patting a captured English child's head. The footage was intended to demonstrate Saddam as a kind 'uncle'—as someone who is warm and approachable, and taking care of his charges. The effect was, however, to present Saddam as a pederast, smiling and perversely enjoying the fear of the child, as he simultaneously touched him on the head. The Iraqi regime had misread the potential moral outrage of the Western audience, and as such, the framing and meaning of Saddam's actions were entirely reversed from the regime's intention. The point of this book is not that the current global media systems present absolute reversibility and relativity as an attribute of events such as the misguided Saddam Hussein episode, but that pivots such as KM can roam across media systems as strange attractors of capital, power and influence. In many ways, the twenty years that have passed between the first Gulf War and the present day have fundamentally changed the contexts in which the media function. New media devices and instant digital production have made access to news ubiquitous, mobile and trans-national. This means that media objects such as KM can potentially have substantial, long-lasting and multitudinous impacts beyond the previous tensions and dualities between the East and the West or Muslim and non-Muslim countries, which I shall explore more fully in chapter 7 of this book in terms of the new forms and contemporary organisational aspects of capitalism that KM as media object relies upon. This form of capitalism requires media events that are connected to world trade and subjectivity, and are comprehensible as algorithms of distribution, consumption and population.

One of the reasons that these algorithms are of interest to us is the backdrop of global financial crisis and environmental ruin upon which capitalist growth is now predicated. This book therefore works in two ways. Firstly, the first six chapters 'fill out' the non-linear history that has gone to make up the contemporary situation with KM as international global media object and the reality of a capitalised education. Such 'filling out' in this book works from within, to describe the pulsions and drivers of the British royal family, their inter-playing with the media and broadcast of status in history, and to demonstrate a particular mode of royal survival and expansion. Secondly, the book should be read as a means to understand how key terms and concepts are reconciled and over-lain, putting immanent materialism to work in terms of describing the movable unit: 'power-reception-learning'. The second point involves a lateral, flat mode of construction, depending on coincidences, similarities, herd-like and exceptional behaviours and the formulation of a ruse. This ruse depends upon the notion that beyond the narrow, human-dominated and controlling power concerns of the British royal family and the domain which they have surveyed, lies the inhuman, unhuman and post-human ways in which economic crisis and environmental disaster are now convergent through a capitalised education. To understand such a convergence one needs an expansive imagination, beyond thoughts of naive empirical patterning, or the direct extrapolation of what has happened on the Earth in the past. The truth is that the end of the human species will not be a simple, painless or unheralded performance. KM as media focus stands as an ironic, absurd and rather strange foregrounding to what is going on behind her latter day rise to pre-eminence. Therefore, the secondary, but vital connections in this book which are formed and understood via and through immanent materialism, draw lines between the absolute nihilism of the last dying gasps of a tired hierarchy, total system and exhausted worldview and its attempts to survive. These connections are like a scene from a Mervyn Peake novel that describes in detail the cob webs in the gables, the infinite fawning gestures, and the irrevocable ceremony through time of a dysfunctional, ruling family. One finally begins to understand the ghost-like existence of the British royal family in all its absurdity and beyond the ruse. The royals are the present-day captains on the metaphorical ship, who are continually trying to normalise the situation, as the whole vessel lurches, tips over, and starts to slide into an icy sea of our own creation. One might say: "Everything will be alright". "We will be saved, after all, we are smart human beings, there is no need to worry—there must be a solution to all this, we must avoid the drowning"...

This book brings together the many threads that underpin KM as media object and a capitalised education through an immanent material analysis of non-linear plateaux. Such an undertaking is the very opposite of a sedentary meandering though progressive historical records, or an academic paper that focuses on one tiny aspect of the edifice that supports KM as media object in our lives and a capitalised education. Rather, the whole is theorised through immanence and materiality, and the ways which they come together though global media audiences, world trade and distinct knowledge economies[7]. At root, this confluence of influences, groupings and powers makes up a mosaic of subjectivity that goes beyond rationally constructed analyses of the contemporary situation. In other words, this book is about: who we are, and who we become, as KM burrows into consciousness, and our perception of her as media object emerges and changes given fresh evidence and the inter-connect-edness of another plateau, and that is backgrounded by the firmament of capitalism:

> No social formation appears to be possible beyond capitalism, which realises in parodic form the immanence that was blocked from realisation in philosophy. If immanence is impossible in philosophy as Lacanian-Althusserians maintain, then it realises itself, almost in revenge, in the ravaging deterritorializations of advanced capitalism[8].

Chapter 1

The fundamentals of capital and learning

[Diana Spencer] 31st of August, 1997

Introduction

I had been working all night on writing a cyberpunk and education Ph.D. chapter[9], when news started to seep through in the early morning hours about a major car accident in Paris. I had been researching and typing on an internet connected PC with an open news channel. At first, the news readers expressed disbelief and astonishment at the incident. The presenters, reading the unfolding news aghast at their desks in London, communicated the thought: "Diana Spencer could not be dead, there must be a mistake". But there was no mistake. Diana Spencer, the recently divorced wife of Charles, the Prince of Wales, had been taken to a hospital in Paris and had died of internal injuries suffered in the car crash. The UK was plunged into shock, people openly mourned; the next few weeks were dominated by the return of her body to England, the unforgettable motor cavalcade with innumerable flowers thrown onto Diana's hearse and her brother's monumental funeral eulogy. The voice of a country rang out with an immutable phrase: "We have lost an angel". But what had we really lost? What does the immanent materialist analysis of this book and the specific plateau constructed around the date of 31st of August, 1997, help us to understand about the situation and beyond?

This chapter represents the plateau of the 31st of August, 1997, and the confluence of intensities and threads which run through that date. The death of Diana Spencer was a pivotal event in the confirmation of the 24-hour news cycle, wherein cable, satellite and terrestrial news coverage demanded stories that had impact and global significance on a 24-hour basis. The death of Diana Spencer was one such event that absorbed and expanded the news channels around the world in a unique and ground-breaking manner. There was a tidal wave of investigation and developing conspiracy theories about how Diana had died, there were replays of her life story and speculation about what would happen to the royal family of Britain and to the harassment of the paparazzi. According to the immanent materialism of this chapter, these intrigues and discourses tell us something about the power concerns at play during this period and the often concealed, but vital formations of capital and learning that were emergent during these global plays for power on the 31st of August, 1997. Capital and learning are central to the 31st of August, 1997, because this date represents a zenith in neoliberal activity in terms of the ways in which 'marketisation' and subjectivity were being united and reinvented in unforeseen and unimaginable ways that will be explored in this chapter. As a co-mingling and concomitance to watching the events of the death of Diana Spencer on the global media, we were simultaneously losing something of our former selves. On the 31st of August, 1997, we lost our innocence to the global media, and with it, we lost a part of our characters that had not previously been wholly riven by 'pan-national' consumerism.

The 'consumerite' princess

The point of this writing is not that we suddenly and irreversibly became dedicated and complete consumers on the 31st of August, 1997, but that the ways in which our behaviours could be altered and affected due to media influence underwent a 'phase change' on and around that date. The narrative of Diana Spencer was subsequently raised to a mythological and 'Disneyfied' level. Diana was a beautiful aristocrat with a good heart, who had married a prince, and who had been betrayed and cruelly cut down in her prime. Diana's story helped to sell Barbie princess dolls, revamped DVDs of Disney classics with fairy tale princesses, and kept us watching the global media coverage of the unfolding espionage, tributes and bemused reactions, and this viewer impact consequently created substantial advertising revenue. The death of Diana had enormous 'media weight'. The biggest impact with reference to this study was to merge capital and learning together as one throughout the global media. This happened because capital flows were now completely aligned with what we were watching on the global media. The only problem with this packaging was that further events were consequently necessary, our subjectivities now required increasing stimulation to keep viewing interest—i.e., 'the death of the princess' had been normalised. After the death of Princess Diana, watching and learning about war, scandal, economic collapse or environmental ruin seemed rather banal and somewhat empty. One could state that 'we missed Diana', and we missed her presence, as perhaps the only thoroughly good member of the British royal family. But what does this statement of longing and loss mean? How could Diana Spencer have endeared herself to the general British public and beyond to such an extent, and what are the consequences in terms of the future media object of Kate Middleton (KM) and her 'capitalised education', that will be explored in depth in chapter 7? One could breakdown the most important elements of the 'consumerite princess' into 3 parts that explain how capital and learning are henceforth convergent and conflated through the specific intensities of the plateau of the 31st of August, 1997:

1   New technology: This was the period of the great 'dot.com' bubble. Neoliberal economic policy in the United States of America and elsewhere (such as the UK) had created an unregulated internet and digital market, which was described by some at the time as the 'new Wild West'. Anything could happen in the 'new Wild West', and what

was happening was a furious and unrelenting investment in digital technological applications and new, mediated forms of communication that were hosted by web sites. Whole networks and regimes of economic activity now shifted into the online, global environment (e.g. Amazon.com). The internet was suddenly and undoubtedly the place to do business and the way to learn about and exploit new business opportunities—even if many of these businesses subsequently went bust after the 'dot.com' crash, creating widespread redundancy!

2   Affect: Diana Spencer was an extremely affective person. She exuded 'likeability' through her combination of good looks, voice, character traits and seeming good will to everyone she met, except perhaps, her husband Prince Charles! Charles was clearly perturbed by this aspect of Diana's demeanour and was frequently overshadowed by her in their public appearances. The affect that Diana produced also explains to some extent the consequent grief and loss that the public felt after her death. Many people felt her death personally, and this was recognised at the time by the capital markets as a new power in global economics. The value of emotion, affect and 'relationality' were reversed over time from being seen as negative, weak and detrimental, to being positive attributes for doing business, seen, for example, in the rise of the fashion industry, and its place in the cultural industries of society. The emerging digitalised global communication system could carry and project affects, and henceforth it was recognised that this system would be a vital sales medium that could directly touch the sentiments and change the minds of the consumer.

3   Hierarchy: The death of Diana Spencer did not herald a sustained clamour for a republic in the UK. On the contrary, her death reinforced the existing hierarchy. The British royal family could once again shrink back from the precipice that

the specific questioning of Diana Spencer had pushed them to, and this change of stance played into the hands of capital and learning. In fact, nothing changed in the hierarchy, Charles continued his affair with Camilla, whom he latterly married, the Queen of Britain continued her reign unabashed and reinforced, the public emotion that had previously been rallied against the royal family by Diana was dissipated and satiated by the particular outpouring of grief for the dead Diana.

The notion of a 'consumerite princess' is born out of the contrast and contradiction between Diana Spencer's actions, lifestyle and persona, and the continued hierarchical status quo in Britain. Global capitalism, which is largely powered by investment strategies on the global markets, accelerated in the gaps between existing capitalised classes and non-capitalised classes. The historic and centuries old capitalist story repeated itself: the rich got richer through free market trade, the poor stayed poor without access to these markets, inequality expanded, and the status quo was reinforced. The 31st of August, 1997 was not a tipping point in terms of social change or revolution, but shows how events such as the death of Diana can have an opposite effect to social progressivism. The consumerism that is connected to the death of Diana and the date of 31st of August, 1997, confirms the fact that dead heroes sell products better than living revolutionaries: e.g., Jimi Hendrix, Jim Morrison, Ché Guevara and James Dean. Diana was no longer a complicated, living actor with particular foibles, limitations and pathos, but she was now a dead object, that could be easily manipulated by living power concerns and incorporated into energetic and global capital flows.

The social contract – a consumer life

The plateau of August the 31st, 1997, brought together significant forces in world history that are characterised in this chapter through the convergence of capital and learning. Tony Blair and Bill Clinton, who were the politicians in power in the UK and the USA, seized on this moment to move their policies to a new 'middle ground'. This middle ground worked due to the ubiquitous investment possibilities that were to be found through globally interconnected capitalism. The next stage in global economics was being unveiled in combination with and through their neoliberal policies, and these developments unfolded, for example, through the narrative of Microsoft. What this meant was an increase in the intensity and possibilities in global capitalism, and more specifically, the signifying signs involved with investment and trade were accelerated and produced by new digital technology and the interconnectivity of previously unknown dimensions. However, this semiotics of exchange, made possible through the internet and significant advances in software capabilities, also required a social contract. People had to 'buy into' these changing conditions, and they must take advantage of what was on offer through the internet. There was no business to be done by Amazon if people all over the world didn't have fast and reliable access to the internet, and the desire to consume what was being sold and exchanged. Therefore, a social contract between the government and its citizens was required in order to expand into the new mediated dimension. This contract involved participation in 'pan-hyper-consumerism', and a suite of governmental policies that enabled such participation[10]. These policies worked through education, as children were introduced to global market conditions through 'consumer pedagogy', see below for further explanation, in the section on neoliberal educational reform. The new consumer policies were broadcast through the media, as the role of advertising increasingly began to dominate any other types of programming. Unemployment, or becoming globally mobile were no barrier to living the consumer life, as credit was cheap and negotiable, and the flows of capitalised debt and repayment could reach you just about anywhere on the planet, except for perhaps in North Korea! The old dreams of dropping out, of being a hippie, of revolutionary action, or living on a commune were exhausted. The neoliberal social contract that underpinned living a consumer life was operationalised, transnational and became the only way to live around and through the plateau of August the 31st, 1997. Yet what does the consumer life mean? How is living this consumer life connected to the death of Diana Spencer?

There is no coincidence that the plateau of this chapter sits upon the extensive cyborg theorisations of the 1990s in cybernetics, the social sciences and cultural theory[11]. The cyborg is a figure of the human invaded by technology. Around the plateau of August the 31st, 1997, digital technology could no longer be discounted as an 'analogue other' to us, which we could readily choose to ignore. Rather, the ways in which digitalisation affected us became written into our DNA to greater extent during this period—the articulation of which could be traced back to the 1980s and William Gibson's cyberpunk. This rewriting and rethinking of the human psyche is a powerful aspect of the plateau of August the 31st, 1997, and can be understood through the media coverage of the death of Diana Spencer. Before her death, the possibility of a human character devoid of digital content was still operant. After the death of Diana, and due to the realisation by the groups who control international media networks of the penetration, power and coverage of such events, the digitalisation of commercial regimes became a feedback system. This meant that any notions of a 'pure human' or of an 'unmediated, authentic experience' were extinguished. Human life was effectively replaced by a suite of cyborg behaviours such as: 'switching on', 'logging in', 'booting up', 'surfing', 'information processing' and passive-active systems of debt, advertising, credit and consumption—all accelerated and mediated by digital networks. Governments had to write into their policy settings the new cyborg necessities, which were translated through educational means into literacy and citizenship programs, and the consequent docility of the body in normative regimes of digital envelopment[12]. Meanwhile, those who could manipulate the capital flows that accompanied the 'cyborgisation' of society through digital systems became extraordinarily rich, along with and according to the new social contract.

The plateau of the 31st of August, 1997, is therefore one wherein the forces of capitalism merged and accelerated according to the principles of digitalism. The social science cyborg theories of this period were often framed as counter narratives to digital submergence and hegemony and the accompanying consumerism. Yet this plateau also personifies the ways in which the notions of counter narrative, discourse and critical assessment of the processes of digitalisation were becoming redundant. This is because the translation of these forms of doing intellectual business in the public arena was also changing; they were precisely being put under pressure due to the conflation of learning and capital in and through digitalisation. Intellectual critiques of the ways in which we were 'becoming cyborg' hold little sway if these critiques have no impact in the online digitised marketplace. Yet by having products 'for sale' in the digital marketplace, or by occupying a position in an institute that is subject to globalised digital competition, one immediately partakes in the cyborg changes that were immanent according to the plateau of the 31st of August, 1997. The immanent materialism of this book offers another way of looking at these cyborg changes, one that does not defy or sublimate their impacts, but subverts the grounds whereby these changes work through the identification, construction and reworking of the plateau. A central aspect of these transformational processes could be characterised as 'cyborg capitalism'.

Cyborg capitalism

The acceleration in capital circulation through global digital networks and the corresponding learning functions, constructs the plateau of the 31st of August, 1997. Through this plateau, digitised and mediated modes of production find new ways to open up and exploit global markets and therefore yield higher profits. The death of Diana Spencer acts as a pivot to these processes and formations, and connects such widespread economic robotics to one identifiable human sacrifice. However, the most penetrating effects of cyborg capitalism are felt through the ways in which absence and distance are now made real to the subject, i.e., the subject is transformed by the digital connectivity available and the new emergent relationships with objects. The point here is not how much we personally miss Diana Spencer, but that global digital connectivity, and the corresponding expansion of subjectivity creates 'black holes' wherein our imaginations and creativity now migrate—called the digital imaginary. Thinking about the death of Diana incorporates all the otherwise disconnected material into such an event. Rather than being a clean break with the past, the death of the princess is a mode of consumerism that capital pours into and exploits as the ramifications in terms of viewing potential became apparent. Cyborg capitalism determines the point at which consumptive behaviours have changed, and the old analogue relationships between workers and owners have been subsumed by the psychological and sociological consequences of moving to the digital economy. These processes, which were energised as a zenith on the 31st of August, 1997, are far from complete, as will be explored further in chapter 7 and with respect to Kate Middleton (KM).

Deleuze and Guattari's two main texts deal with the negative effects of capitalism in terms of schizophrenia[13]. In the first text, the tendency towards schizophrenia that is determined by being dominated and manipulated by capitalist modes of production is 'solved' through 'schizoanalysis', which is a type of reverse psychoanalysis that liberates the revolutionary energies locked up by in the schizo position. In the second text, the field of operation is intellectually dispersed and historicised, in order to make use of the ways in which the revolutionary forces that one may liberate from schizophrenia are not 're-subjectivised'. This deliberate convolution relates to 'cyborg capitalism' in terms of escape routes from the ways in which digitalisation creates an immanent plane of operation. These 'lines of flight' are also present in the term 'assemblage' which is arguably one of the most important theoretical constructions of *1000 Plateaus*, and defines a way of thinking about cyborg capitalism that is directly relevant to this chapter. The assemblage is an emergent and chaotic collection of 'things', both human and non-human, and in the case of cyborg capitalism relates to the ways in which cybernetic networks intermingle with human behaviours and intentions. For example, prospective 'e-entrepreneurs' can borrow capital, go online and construct their businesses, which may or may not succeed. In so doing, their subjectivities and dreams are now related in a complex way to the electronic networks that now carry these thoughts and desires. Such a connection carries on when the 'e-entrepreneurs' are asleep or away from their computers, and defines a new type of linkage which may be profitably understood through the notion of assemblage. The internet does not define a purely digital type of oedipal attachment for the e-entrepreneurs, although oedipalisation is not excluded from internet functioning, but is a complicated mixture of material and market processes, intentions, desires and hopes. The most perspicuous example of the new type of attachment or assemblage that characterises cyborg capitalism is represented by the ways in which the e-entrepreneur now becomes hooked on checking to see the number of web site hits, sales and any consequent revenue that their web site has produced. Such ubiquitous 'checking' behaviour defines a new mode of capital accumulation connected to the cyborg tendencies of the mind, and is immanent through the plateau of August the 31st, 1997.

Perhaps such 'checking' explains in part why the death of Diana Spencer was so powerful. The 'checking' of cyborg capitalism introduces a repetitive, iterative process into consciousness, which potentially weakens the subject, and makes it vulnerable to the type of emotional outpouring in outside events such as the death of Diana Spencer. In contrast to, for example, the processes of making a work or art, or of writing a novel, cyborg capitalism introduces discrete elements into consciousness that determine and potentially limit the ways in which the creative unconscious may function. Rather than strengthening and enhancing the imaginary aspects of the mind, cyborg capitalism delimits and excludes the ways in which one works through fantasy as 'other'. The integrated processes of cyborg capitalism therefore signify a narrowing and limiting of the mind according to the analysis of this chapter. In contrast to a straightforward Marxist critique of cyborg capitalism in terms of digital ownership and the means of production of 'cyborg consumer markets', the immanent materialism of this book extends a complex analysis of the situation, both objective and subjective, to deliver a new vision of subjectivity based on the conditions of cyborg capitalism that work through the plateau of the 31st of August, 1997. The result is a plural and flexible means to resist and question the ways in which cyborg capitalism henceforth dominates our behaviour and learning. In many ways, immanent materialism asks us to use the conditioning of cyborg capitalism against itself in order to unlearn the fundamentals of consumerism, and the accompanying debt relationships that enslave us. In other words, it is 'OK' to understand and feel the irrational affect of Diana's death, but this feeling state must be extended and used in order to open up the immanent and material conditions that the death of Diana has produced in the new stage of global capitalism. Such extension and usage is a highly imaginative and creative act, as well as requiring focused rationality.

It is precisely this usage of irrationality that some commentators have questioned with respect to Deleuze and Guattari's analysis[14]. One could ask: Why don't we stick to a simply rational analysis of capitalism and the ways that it affects us? The major problem with only employing a rational analysis of capitalism is that such intellectual work precisely misses out on the irrational, unconscious forces that are immanent through the framing and functioning of capitalism. The plateau of August the 31st, 1997, includes such energetics, and extends them in this analysis. Cyborg capitalism is a construction that attempts to explain and exemplify the ways in which the systems and forms in our dominant social systems were transformed through the combinations of digitalism and neoliberal policy in and around this period. In contrast to temporally linear, power based critiques of capitalism, which locate and determine forms of alienation, worker-owner-labour relations, surplus and use value, etc., immanent materialism constructs a specific plateau through which the digitalisation of capitalism may be understood and subverted. Cyborg capitalism defines a 'human/non-human' feedback system, and a multiplicity of factors running through this system, that were enmeshed and accelerated through the plateau of August the 31st, 1997 as capital and learning. One of the most important of these factors is present in nihilism[15].

Humans can believe in God, the beauty of nature, salvation, reincarnation, revolution or a host of animist notions about the world, society and the human self. In contrast, capital flows from between banks, private investors, companies and governments in order to build new businesses or to speculatively invest in the future, and to make a profit as the only belief by anyone involved in the enterprise. This system of capital flows achieved a phase change in and around the plateau of the 31st of August, 1997, through advancements in digital software technology and the internet. As such, human belief of the kind mentioned above was put under direct pressure by global capitalism and consumerism. Of course, one could still personally choose to believe in God, the point is that these beliefs were now directly in relation to, and in competition with the ways in which consumerist global capitalism aligned with digital technology could dominate the world as a set of beliefs. New automatic machines around the world could invest in an international plurality of markets at immense speeds, increasing the likelihood of capital flow, 'hyper'-consumerism and fiscal reciprocity, and as will be seen in chapter 7, these processes have not ceased. These cyborg capitalist formations of the plateau have led to a new notion of nihilism[16], or belief in nothing, that subsumes and consumes other beliefs in its radius. The argument here is not that the new form of cyborg materialism is opposed to spirituality, or that the world has become less religious since the plateau of August the 31st, 1997, but that there is a new and evolving relationship between pre-digital modes of belief and the ways in which cyborg capitalism affects us. This relationship opens up a new mode of thinking about pre-digital modes of belief, that have been described, for example, in the work of Eugene Thacker as a type of demonology[17].

Horror and demonology

One of the most interesting aspects of the plateau of the 31st of August, 1997, is the ways in which it develops a relationship with the unconscious. Beyond the specific affect of grief that was induced across a large swath of the UK population due to the death of Diana Spencer, there was an unprecedented opportunity to learn about and apply forms of the occult through the opening up of the internet. The 'new Wild West' was not only an opportunity to do global business, but it was a means to expose previously undiscussed or suppressed matters such as pre-modern modes of belief. The argument here is not that we all suddenly became animists, devil worshippers, witches or shamans around the plateau of the 31st of August, 1997, but that these thoughts are immanent to it workings. The result is a form of horror and demonology, a translated and updated mode of the occult, which is relevant and pertinent to the plateau. Cyborg capitalism works in many directions and in many forms, not only to extend the profits of capitalised e-entrepreneurs, but also to expose a new type of nihilism. This is the other side of capital and learning, a 'dark side' which was in a state of intense acceleration at the same time as corporate global capitalism became entirely dominant. A personal example to demonstrate the truth of this statement came in the free party, rave movement of the 1990s in the UK, and the ways in which this movement potentially induced 'techno-shamanism'.

Going to a free party and dancing all night to techno music in secret locations, is just about as opposite a behaviour to sitting in a corporate office during the working, 9am-5pm, day and performing for a corporation, as one can imagine. Yet these behaviours were sitting side-by-side and on top of each other during the 1990s in the UK. Margaret Thatcher's 1980s right wing government had passed specific laws during the last days of her dying regime that had legislated against groups of more than a certain number of individuals dancing to repetitive beats (25 people maximum). As far as I am aware, this is the only legislation of such a kind in the world, and was spurred on by England's sedentary and capitalised middle classes, who had backed the Tory government for 12 years. The effect of the legislation was to push the free party movement into an illegal underground existence—and in many ways this specific law increased the intensity and popularity of the subterranean parties. The arrival of the internet in the 1990s provided a new means to organise. I joined the legions of the free party movement during my Ph.D. studies, and specifically when I became a lodger for an aristocratic family with property and land in the Midlands of the UK. The young aristocrat whose property I was looking after had reconstructed an old outer barn as an art gallery, which coincidentally served as a great party venue. I was involved with a collective of young DJs and became, by chance, their *de facto* leader.

Techno-shamanism wasn't the official religion or title for the practice of free partying. Rather, the notion of techno-shamanism comes through the rave as an immanent aspect of its existence and reality. Techno-shamanism is about becoming, it is about the ways in which technology can be used to alter consciousness[18]. There was a definite collective power involved with the raves, and one which is difficult to express fully in language. The rave is a bodily experience, even when accompanied by the 'spacey otherness' that repetitive beats and a powerful sound system can induce. The shaman in hunter and gatherer societies entered a deliberately augmented psychic state in order to have visions for the tribe, for healing purposes and to usefully predict the future. The belief in the powers of the shaman was clear to the tribe by the success or otherwise of his practises, and not routed through belief in God or any transcendent experience. Rather, the shaman became one with the body of the tribe and proved his worth, or was ostracised. The same could be said about the free party raves. Once dance music 'went commercial' and was relocated from the remaining folds of the English countryside to enormous glitzy nightclubs, something vital was lost, the shamanism of the dance died. The occult only works as a secret, as something non-exploitative or hidden. The vulgar commercial interest in the rave killed its energy, and condemned the experience to the bland repetitions and clichés of commercial culture.

The trace of the free parties that one would immanently describe for the plateau of the 31st of August, 1997, corresponds to the horror and demonology that one may extract from the experience. Such a depiction is not necessarily a negative assessment of the free parties, but deliberately avoids the 'new age' idealism that one might want to suggest with respect to these celebrations. For the purposes of this book, and the immanent materialism that one may derive from Deleuze and Guattari's *1000 Plateaus,* the illegal rave parties that traverse the plateau of the 31st of August, 1997 are forms of collective behaviour that tell us something radically different about the effects of cyborg capitalism other than and complementary to the corporate and capital enmeshing with the digital processes. In the corporate sphere, the ways in which greed, power and the profit motive are activated and extended by cyborg capitalism take precedence. In the illegal party sphere, a form of demonology and horror inhabits the space, and this inhabitation extends to the ways in which the atmosphere of the rave defines a new type of learning. The full 'shamanology' of the rave is a cross-over effect that could take hold in the corporate sphere if a portal between the two is successfully constructed and activated. Perhaps this writing is an attempt to figure such a bridge, as the true horror of a corporate take-over of life through cyborg capitalism becomes apparent in terms of global warming, irreversible urbanisation, the GFC (see chapter 7). Of course, the two sides of cyborg capitalism described in this section, i.e., the [corporate/rave] material complex are not designed to reinstate a form of dualism, or any resultant judgements about adverse and augmented effects of cyborg capitalism. Rather, the immanent materialist analysis of this book, works in terms of the objects of corporatisation and the subjects of the rave becoming inter-changeable and moving on the same plane.

Commentators may negatively question the theoretical and conceptual move taken from the philosophy of Deleuze and Guattari with respect to the interchangeability of subject and objects[19], but this aspect of the writing is essential to understand how the political and ontological aspects of immanent materi-alism work. Contrast such an approach to, for example, a forensic examination of the facts of corporate life and rave life, under the influence of cyborg capitalism and through the plateau of the 31st of August, 1997. A forensic approach separates and categorises the ways in which corporate life and the rave life work. Immanent materialism figures the [corporate/rave] transverse unit as a multiplicity of flows that creep their ways into the 'giveness of things'. The plateau of the 31st of August, 1997, acts as plane, whereupon different elements function and inter-relate, recognisable in the conscious and unconscious working of things. Perhaps the full 'shamanology' of the plane is an especially unconscious or submerged aspect of the plateau of the 31st of August, 1997, but it is one that should be nonetheless recognised as the horror and demonology of its existence becomes apparent. A good example to demonstrate how immanent materialism works, and one that conjoins the thinking behind these remarks about [corporate/rave] complexity, is in the reorganisation of the education systems of post-industrial countries such as the UK, USA and Australia around and through the plateau of the 31st of August, 1997. Digital technology and the internet heralded unprecedented possibilities for educational reform in the 1990s, which were implemented in what one might call, neoliberal terms.

Neoliberal educational reform

Capital and learning were being aligned and conflated through governmental policy in the 1990s, as the realisation of a new stage of capitalism, explained in this chapter as 'cyborg capitalism', was immanent. Market reforms and the neoliberal (capitalist) agenda in education had been ongoing before the 31st of August, 1997, but the plateau of this chapter saw an enormous acceleration in the ways in which market solutions to educational reform were enacted. At the same time that Diana Spencer died, schools, school districts, universities and many places of learning were undergoing reforms according to the principles of how markets function and corporate design pressure. These processes included: the standardised testing of students in subjects such as literacy and mathematics; performance pay for teachers based largely on the results of standardised testing; inspection regimes and new levels of bureaucracy to check and publish the particular practises of schools and universities; the regularisation of university research practices through citation indexing and the assessment of faculties and departments through comparative indexed publications; the publication of professional standards for teachers and lecturers; the tendency towards universal, standard curricula, published and administered by a centralised bureaucracy; increased feedback and pedagogic assessment mechanisms for students, teachers and lecturers through questionnaires, surveys, quantitative research and electronic means; the translation of all educational modes to a form of assessable, market-based 'training'. I could probably extend this list substantially, given the suite of neoliberal reforms that were enacted during this period and afterwards. Some of these measures have been since repealed due to negative educational effects that have been observed and researched on the ground, and the efforts of mainly qualitative and critical researchers, whilst other neoliberal reforms have intensified in scope and penetration to accelerate cyborg capitalism. The overall result of these reforms has been to extend corporate modes of working into educational life, producing a form of 'pedagogy of the consumer' as has been previously mentioned.

The coordinated and combined effects of the 'pedagogy of the consumer' are to turn the subject into a consumer from an early age. The new digital economies of Western democracies demand strongly emergent domestic consumption to support an expanded retail sector. This growth has to be in coordination with fiscal policy, manufacturing and service businesses, knowledge production and distribution, and international export and import trade. The importance of consumerism and

27

consumer sentiment therefore rose significantly during and around the plateau of the 31st of August, 1997, and this often sublimated, unconscious message begins at school. Knowledge effectively became a commodity to be traded, knowledge transmission and production had to be coordinated and controlled along economic lines. Such a shift in pedagogic focus towards consumerism in knowledge content came in conjunction with the reorganisation of educational facilities along corporate lines. This reorganisation effectively took control of the body of education, and made any exceptionality to these new ways of working harder to imagine around and through the plateau of this chapter. Of course, one could still posit a generalised 'anti-capitalist pedagogy' that could directly oppose and work against the incursion of consumerism into pedagogic practice[20]. Yet the ways in which neoliberal market forces work makes complete opposition almost impossible to sustain. Rather, the immanent materialism of this book follows the ebbs and flows of consumerism in educational thought, both conscious and unconscious, and in so doing opens up new ways of figuring the normative processes of educational consumerism that are implied by the plateau of the 31st of August, 1997.

The complex [corporate/rave] unit that was figured above according to the philosophy of immanent materialism works at the level of the 'consumer normative' in learning and capital by opening up and realigning subjectivity. Teachers, students and lecturers who have been invaded by the ways in which cyborg capitalism introduces waves of consumer thought and practice into their lives, have an escape route through the [corporate/rave] synthetic combination. The multiple options that the [corporate/rave] unit gives the user go beyond the notion of choice offered by neoliberalism or 'the market'. For example, a group or collective may attend to the learning capabilities and forms necessary to make a circus of street performance function and succeed today[21]. Such coordinated teaching and learning practice rarely happens in mainstream schools, because this type of open and speculative practice goes beyond the functional and market based expectations of what knowledge is and how it should be taught and learnt in contemporary schooling dominated by standardised testing. However, many of the skills, technical abilities and ways in which knowledge works with respect to circus and street performance, are directly relevant to the workplace today. Perhaps such a 'unit of work' could be fitted in with the corporatized learning outcomes and pre-defined pedagogic practices that are currently in place in schools in terms of the creative arts. However, the imagination, creativity and skill to put together the music, performance skills, narrative, tricks and marketing expertise for the circus of street performers to succeed, go beyond most current forms of integrated curriculum. This unit of work would require a level of cooper-ation, integrity and action that circumvents a transmission model of knowledge. The student and teacher are implemented in the scenario, in such a way as to productively negate the effects of choice or 'buy in' with respect to the knowledge and curriculum on offer, as if they were objects to be consumed. The [corporate/rave] unit—as demonstrated by the street performer circus—is an affective and powerful means to work with the effects of capital and learning that run through this chapter and the neoliberal reforms in education.

The circus of street performers is a good example to show how immanent materialism works. Rather than having to set up an alternative 'anti-neoliberal' school, the educators running the street circus lessons can work inside the existing education system, but subvert the functioning from within, and not enter into explicitly oppositional relationships with the tenets and defenders of neoliberalism. Of course, opposition may occur, as it does with respect to any innovative practice, yet immanent materialism is a flexible philosophical perspective, which can embrace and work around direct opposition and those who wish to preserve the system as it currently exists, including the raft of neoliberal policy measures that coincide with the plateau of the 31st of August, 1997. Below the surface of explicit sets of reforms, such as neoliberal education policy, lie the deeper and political ways in which society works, where beliefs, thoughts and sentiments mingle with the new modes of working in society, described as cyborg capitalism in this chapter. Cyborg capitalism is not a wellspring for conservatism or reactivity against the modes of working as represented, for example, by the street performer circus, but takes these forms of action and accelerates their functioning according to the principles of the cybernetics that determine the 'becoming-cyborg'. The [corporate/rave] unit as described above, may be inserted into the ways in which the circus of street performers work, and used to protect the activity against the detrimental effects of 'becoming-cyborg' such as digital submergence. This protective effect happens because the drives involved with any particular actions, e.g. the preparation and enactment of a street circus, are enhanced and extended by the [corporate/rave] entity. Deleuze and Guattari might call the [corporate/rave] unit an abstract machine, as it works from within to allay outside influences, such as the immanent 'becoming-cyborg' of cyborg capitalism. One of the most dramatic outside influences and effects of the plateau of the 31st of August, 1997, was the 'death of a princess' wherein the conflation of capital and learning was possible.

The death of a princess

The online funeral oration of Earl Spencer about the death of his sister[22], has subsequently 'gone viral' since 1997, with the help of the internet, global media networks and students studying the speech as part of their pre-tertiary English courses. In the speech, the Earl painted a brilliantly sympathetic picture of his sister, and the ways in which she had become an absolute object of media attention "in the modern age", and as has happened to her successor, Kate Middleton (KM) and as shall be explored further in chapter 7. The meaning of the 'death of a princess' is here transplanted into the plateau of the 31st of August, 1997, which includes a new phase of capitalism, called cyborg capitalism in this chapter and that exists with an accompanying plane of nihilism, which transforms the 'death of a princess' through 'unmeaning'. Such 'unmeaning' is vital, as it is tempting to be overridden by affect, and a particular, emotional response to Diana's death. Yet there is a colder, less personal side to the 'death of a princess', which has been examined here through global consumerism and is played out in the politics of neoliberal educational reform. The plateau of the 31st of August, 1997, sees an unprecedented merging of capital and learning, as the ways in which digital technology relates to subjectivity were beginning to be understood and the exploitation of cyberspace effectively moved into a different gear. This new gearing allowed for the full realisation of global capitalism and the ways in which trade could become immanent to the subject and its desires.

The immanent materialist philosophy of this book requires the affect of the 'death of a princess' to build and understand the plateau that works around such an historic event. The challenge here is to intellectually manipulate the ways in which the death of Diana moved the world. The affect involved with the 'death of a princess' can become personal, psychological and inwardly mixed up with grief, pity and cynicism about the stasis of the ruling hierarchy. Yet this affect can simultaneously release the energy necessary to explore the plateau as an unknown territory, or as an object that is exciting and new. The creative unconscious begins to work as a thinking process as the immanence of the plateau begins to become apparent. This chapter has attempted to work on this level, as if one is able to pull back the curtains on the 'death of a princess' and discover a previously unknown world, populated by cyborg capitalism, nihilism, consumer pedagogy and the accelerated conflation of capital and learning.

Just as the speech of Earl Spencer works to give us a strongly emotional and personal connection with the death of his sister, Diana Spencer, the words and ideas of this chapter work from within to produce a mapped territory of the emergent plateau of the 31st of August, 1997. Of course, the ways in which these processes work differ subjectively as reading itself can bring different factors to bear on the matters at hand[23].

One could say, "I don't care about the death of a princess", but this dead end in thought misses the point of the construction of the plateau of the 31st of August, 1997. The point here is that our emotional and unconscious reactions to events such as the 'death of a princess', were being processed through cyborg capitalism as a result of the workings of the plateau. Even individuals living in North Korea, where the state government controlled all information access in 1997, and where capitalism was strongly framed as the enemy to everything good in life, would begin to come into direct contact with global consumerist values, as the population in neighbouring China changed its direction and progressively inculcated Western capitalist mores into its collective functioning. The plateau of the 31st of August, 1997, figures the likelihood of alternatives to the global domination of capitalism as increasingly impossible. Mark Fisher has asserted this fundamental question with respect to the future of human society as representing 'capitalist realism'[24]. This chapter and book about the capitalised education of Kate Middleton, also frame such a question, but through immanent materialism, which as has been argued in the introduction, incurs a new politics into the equation. A realist approach to understanding capitalism could productively open up epistemological and intellectual questions about the continuing reality of global capitalism. However, realism does not construct the plateaux that define the immanence of the situation, in this chapter, with respect to the death of Diana Spencer. More specifically, realism could miss the unconscious elements of global trade that spark and redefine the ways in which capitalism now affects us. In chapter 7, which focuses on the reality of Kate Middleton (KM) as media object, these elements will be brought up to date and intensified, as cyborg capitalism is left behind, and new mobile technology breaks up any previously held belief in the unified aspects of the self.

The plateau of the 31st of August, 1997, frames the 'death of a princess' as something immanent and powerful, and attempts to subvert the affective grounds that could turn this event into a 'black hole' of thought. Earl Spencer could eloquently express the emotions involved with the death of his sister, as his affective literacy skills processed the feelings of grief, loss and bewilderment and turned these emotions into language with sustained and widespread impact. In this chapter, the formative elements of the 'death of a princess' have been brought out, described and synthesised due to the principles of immanent materialism. Diana's untimely death connected with the specific conditions necessary for accelerated cyborg capitalism to function, and this functionality worked in unison and resonated with particular social processes, such as neoliberal educational reform. The car crash in a Parisian tunnel did not cause the immanent changes in global capitalism or specific educational reforms, but 'locked in' with them in a chaotic, emergent and complementary fashion. These changing conditions of the plateau are flows that define power relationships and differentials, for example, between citizens and governments, teachers and students, or a princess and the public. One might complain from a deterministic perspective that the philosophy of immanent materialism does not produce scientifically valid results or immutable categories to understand. Yet immanent materialism does produce a new form of politics that takes account of the complex ways in which we relate to and perform with respect to events such as the death of Diana Spencer.

Conclusion

One could argue that this plateau coheres most closely with chapter 7 and the plateau of April the 29th, 2011—the royal wedding. However, the intervening five plateaux add weight and direction to the connection between the death of Diana Spencer and the royal wedding of 2011 and the emergence of KM as media object and a capitalised education. Multi-directional weight and flow are added to the connection between the first and last chapters of this book, through the ways in which one may understand immanent materialism and its underpinnings in this book. For example, the royal aspects of the thesis are emboldened through chapters 2, 3 and 6, the political argumentation is reinforced through chapter 5, and chapter 4 addresses the non-human, machine elements of the argument. However, it is also true that many of the processes, concepts and ideas that have been set up in this chapter are resonant throughout chapter 7, which in many ways extends and deepens their stories. For example, the notion of cyborg capitalism is intensified and accelerated through the finance capitalism of chapter 7, and the [corporate/rave] unit of this chapter is twisted into and through the occupy movement, that includes elements of celebration and festival into surrounding corporate space. Therefore, empirical evidence and the theoretical construction of concepts function in unison throughout this book to ultimately connect KM as media object with all previous plateaux. The shadow of the death of Diana is strong in the construction of KM as media object, yet this powerful augmentation is only part of the story.

Chapter 2

Whose education?

King George VI—The King's Speech
September 3rd, 1939

Introduction

Fifty eight years before the death of Diana Spencer and the tenets of cyborg capitalism and neoliberal educational reform became imaginable, many of the central aspects of a 'capitalised education' that come to fruition with Kate Middleton (KM) as a media object were already being played out. The second constructed plateau of this book works around just such an instance, and the king's speech of September the 3rd, 1939. This analogue speech was transmitted on the radio by the British Broadcasting Corporation, and was meant to reach the population of the 'British Commonwealth of nations' as they are referred to in the speech[25]. This speech was a pivotal war communication and a call to arms for the peoples of British Commonwealth who stood on the brink of global conflict. Yet as has been brilliantly portrayed in the recent film, 'The King's Speech', the king was an extremely reluctant public speaker, who suffered from a crippling stutter that made the delivery of this historic speech of world significance extremely difficult. In terms of the immanent materialism of this book, the specific king's subconscious is reconciled as and through the notion of 'the collective unconscious' to allow for greater openness and a social plane of becoming to emerge in the specific psychological-cultural-power based factors that would have inhibited the king from talking clearly. At the time, theories of the unconscious were not well developed in the UK, even though the influences of Freud and Jung had to a certain extent reached across the

English Channel. The Australian speech therapist, Lionel Logue, took an improvised, quasi-Freudian approach to treating the king's suppressed fears and encouraging the monarch to speak more freely and confidently by, for example, allowing him to openly swear.

However, this chapter is not just a mapping of the specific psychoanalytic terrain that is relevant to the king. To enact the unconscious field of the king's speech, and one that works according to the principles of immanent materialism, the analysis of the plateau of the 3rd of September, 1939, focuses on the material flows, strands and immanent forces that were latterly transformed through the conflation of capital and learning in consumerism, and ultimately into a 'capitalised education' by the time of Kate Middleton (KM). In and through the plateau of the king's speech, which was broadcast on the September the 3rd, 1939, learning and capital were objects that primarily obeyed the laws of class, hence the title of the chapter: Whose Education? This meant that when the king spoke to 'all of us' in the British Commonwealth, the radio message was divided according to class and to location. For example, my grandparents would have listened to the speech in utter horror with respect to their coming fate and the unfolding events in terms of the danger to their East End of London tenement. In contrast, aristocrats in England would have been reassured by the ways in which the king had managed to set aside his awful stammering and delivered this important message that could potentially galvanise the Commonwealth and help to fight the impending war. The middle classes and multitudinous peoples of the Commonwealth would have listened to the speech with a mixture of trepidation, fear and wonder at the tone and linguistic delivery of the king. If one listens to the speech carefully online, one can still hear the vocal problems that "Bertie" experienced, and one is immediately drawn in to the subjectivity of a rather frail and lonely individual.

Royal stuttering

Gilles Deleuze uses the expression of 'to stutter' in several places in his oeuvre with reference to language use[26]. Deleuze was inspired to deploy this expression in his work because of his interest in the ways in which Samuel Beckett and other artists have played with and deliberately cut up or repeated language, or made expression beyond language viable. 'Stuttering' is therefore in the Deleuzian mode an artistic vision, it is a deliberate strategy to make the audience aware that there is expression beyond language, and this expression can be bodily, political, relational, machinic or animal. King George the VI didn't have to deliberately play with or alter his language use to prompt understanding of the expression behind his words. On the contrary, the subjectivity of the man is all too painful and apparent. In the film, 'The King's Speech', there is an attempt to explain the cause of Bertie's stammering with reference to his weak character and linguistic learning problems, his domineering and authoritarian royal father, and through the relationship with his charismatic and articulate elder brother. Yet with respect to the construction of the plateau of September the 3rd, 1939, the representation of lack and emphasis in the subjectivity of the king is not the primary focus of analysis. Henceforth, the particular factors involved with the subjectivity of King George the VI, which are extremely apparent throughout the film of the 'The King's Speech', are explored and expanded in this chapter from an inter-connected perspective that is immanent, flat and burgeoning. I would contend that such a treatment is in line with Deleuze and Guattari's philosophy in *1000 Plateaus,* and that takes stammering seriously, not as a psychoanalytic lack, but as a significant marker in the collective unconscious of a 'capitalised education'. This demarcation takes the form of three 'leaky' meta-levels or strata that conform to the class system of the social pyramid of the 3rd of September, 1939:

1) Stuttering amongst the English speaking, 'working or lower' classes of Britain, was not a significant factor in their lives. Education amongst these classes was not widespread as the plateau of the 3rd of September, 1939, happened before the free comprehensive and secondary modern education movements in the UK took hold in the 1960s. The 'working or lower' classes represented the majority of the population, and were primarily and unfairly valued for their physical labour and skills, which did not require specific literacy or oratory skills. The analysis of the radio broadcast of the king's speech from this perspective was therefore in terms of the imminent facts of total mobilisation, conscription, jobs, housing and food. The male population in Britain had been particularly put under pressure since the carnage of the previous war, and this depletion in male British soldiers made mobilisation of the whole Commonwealth vital. The message of the king's speech was designed to reach all Commonwealth countries, and was translated to help with the mobilisation of non-English speaking soldiers. The relaying of the king's speech through translation therefore further negated the importance of stammering, as the words of the speech were in an imperial foreign language to the overseas listeners.

2) Educated, English speaking, 'middle class' people in Britain and the Commonwealth would have been terrifically conscious of the king's stammer and the implications in terms of power and language. This second strata of the 3rd of September, 1939, is the most familiar in our retrospective view of the plateau. Since that time, the factors relating to the changes and raising of consciousness that mass education has produced—for example, greater class and global mobility, and the conflation of capital and learning through consumerism as has been discussed in chapter 1 has contributed to an intensified perspective on the king's stutter.

One could say that we have become amateur speech thera-
pists, able to analyse and speculate on the processes of
stammering that are apparent in the king's speech. Listeners
of the second strata in Britain and beyond would have been
affectively moved and alerted to the subjective problems of
the king by his speech. In and through this stratum,
cognitive ability was paramount over physical labour, and
any defect in speech could be fatal for job security or status
in the established yet mutable capitalist order. The king's
speech would therefore have provoked a mixture of
credulity, approbation and wonder as to the king's fitness to
deliver such a vital message across the airwaves. The second
stratum of the plateau must have fiercely debated the king's
ability to be the figurehead of the British war effort given his
serious speech problems.

3)   The inhabitants of the remnants of the British aristocracy
and their ostensibly pre-capitalist, 'feudal' social system in
1939 would have been reassured, yet somewhat anxious
with respect to the king's stammer. The recent introduction
of mass radio communication made events such as the radio
message of the monarch to the Commonwealth a window
into a previously closed and protected world. The Second
World War was in some respects an attempt to protect the
aristocratic worldview, led by one of their own, Winston
Churchill. Yet the forces of capitalism, that were enhanced
by the growing power of the United States of America, had
seriously begun to challenge the hegemony and dominion of
the aristocracy, and these forces belong to the second
stratum in this immanent materialist analysis of the 3rd of
September, 1939. Of course, the British aristocracy were
completely involved with and related to the other two strata
in a complex manner through the ways in which the power
and importance of trade and commerce had been increasing
for at least four hundred years. Yet the British aristocracy

still laid claim to traditional hereditary, religious and blood power and rites through their continued domination of land ownership and the evocation of a quasi-mystical, God-given status. For example, if one looks at the contemporary portraits of King George the VI, he is depicted as an imperial ruler, the last emperor, and entirely free of any speech impediment. Yet in 'real life' he was a rather shy, oedipalised and domesticated individual, who loved his family above all else and is the very opposite of a warrior-king.

These precise tensions and contradictions of power are still resonant today, but with respect to the 'capitalised education' of Kate Middleton (KM). Kate was born into the second social stratum as described above, yet has been able to enter the protected confines of the British aristocracy, due to her family taking financial advantage of online developments in 'cyborg capitalism' and henceforth sending Kate to an aristocratic school and university due to their cyber-profits and possible inheritance money (see chapter 7). Kate's social success emphasises and strengthens the British royal family's claim to power by converging with the capitalist imaginary, and with the dreams of wealth and power that this imaginary projects. King George the VI's image and the traditional power of his royal regalia, masked the stammer that was apparent in his speech or in 'real life'. However, the imperial image of the emperor, George the VI, played into the capitalist imaginary by projecting a stable and immutable notion of power, a notion that could be identified with, reproduced or mimicked. In effect, the tension between the rise of the capitalist classes and the British aristocratic order was diminished through the 'happy accident' of deploying a stuttering king as the aristocratic spokesperson. This king could be easily identified with by the first two strata listed above as a 'struggling battler', as someone who was overcoming severe disadvantage to do a good job. Part of the king's job was to protect the aristocratic worldview as has been mentioned above, but he also had to make sure that world capitalism and capital flows survived the serious challenges to their existence and power in terms of the rise of fascism and communism (see chapter 5). In economic terms, one of the most important international capital flows of the plateau of the 3rd of September, 1939, involved tobacco, cigarette production and all connected businesses. In terms of immanent materialism and the plateau of this chapter, the tobacco trade simultaneously relates to the workings of global capitalism, and also to the specifics of the royal stutter, because the king was, unexceptionally, a heavy smoker. Furthermore, the sending of millions of soldiers and personnel to their death to fight against the threat of anti-capitalism was framed in traditional, nationalistic terms, and the cancerous effects of smoking were barely recognised or understood at the time. In consequence, the effects on the three strata in terms of the immanent materialist analysis of this plateau and the combined power of the tobacco trade may be reconciled and demarcated through the 'tobacco death-wish'.

The tobacco death-wish

One of the most powerful and universal aspects of the 'tobacco death-wish' is that it does not discriminate, but affects all three of the strata of the 3rd of September, 1939, alike. In the film, 'The King's Speech', physicians had even recommended that Bertie smoke to help to relieve and relax the physical causation of his stuttering. Indeed, tobacco cigarette smoking was strongly associated with a healthy lifestyle at the time, as is especially portrayed in cigarette advertising[27]. German doctors and scientists had established a statistical correlation between tobacco smoking and lung cancer through years of detailed research prior to 1939, yet this numerical link was not universally accepted or understood beyond the German scientific circles. An approximately twenty year cycle must be studied to understand the correlation between the numbers of cigarettes smoked per person and the incidents of lung cancer, because this is the time taken for lung cancer to become deadly, and which peaked around 1970 in the USA[28]. Therefore, the health effects of the tobacco industry in terms of the inhalation of nicotine into the lungs were not understood in and through the plateau of the 3rd of September, 1939. Rather, tobacco smoking caused an unconscious, yet physiological and repetitive desire for cigarettes, cigars or pipes to become apparent in the subject, and that led to nicotine addiction, the sales of tobacco products and capital flows for the tobacco companies and their shareholders, and subsequent health problems in the body of the subject that evolve through time and the continued smoking of tobacco. This cycle summarises the 'tobacco death-wish'.

The 'tobacco death-wish' sits underneath the plateau of the 3rd of September the 3rd, 1939, as an unconscious marker to the ways in which this plateau is deadly. The very sounds of the king's speech on the radio were infused with tobacco because he was a heavy smoker, his actual words are a call to arms and a declaration of war against anti-capitalist and anti-tobacco trade forces, the air molecules in the room spaces across the Commonwealth would have been permeated with tobacco smoke as people puffed and listened to the speech in their homes. The form of immanence that the 'tobacco death-wish' created in this plateau is therefore striking—such immanence potentially works in a complex way on all external and internal levels. We are only now able to gain a clear, retrospective, rear-view vision through the cigarette smoke, due to the influences of current day medical research and the widespread dissemination of knowledge about the effects of smoking. Contrariwise, in and through the plateau of the 3rd of September, 1939, the cloudiness of the smoke works in terms of binding together the words and messages of the speech, the subjectivity of the king, and the effects of the speech in terms of, for example, troop mobilisation. Nobody knew who would win the upcoming war, or the precise effects of smoking at the time, all that was known was that the king had declared war, that smoking was ubiquitous and socially acceptable, and that there would be mass death. We might wonder now why people couldn't see through this dense 'smoke-screen' and rebel against the message of the king's speech and not march to war. One could suggest that the immanence of the 'tobacco death-wish' acted as a pacifier and an ironic means to quell such rebellion.

One could take a crudely Freudian interpretation of the mass appeal of smoking cigarettes and look at the subconscious, individual, oral satisfaction embedded in the process of smoking. Freud was himself a heavy smoker, and died of a smoking related cancerous infection. However, his psychoanalytic story of the ways in which the unconscious drives could play out in the subjectivity of the smoker, does not fully explain how the immanence of the plane of the 3rd of September, 1939 works. Immanent materialism does not function in terms of individualised psychological or instinctual factors with respect to, for example, smoking. Rather, one gains an overview of the specific yet complex factors involved with what made smoking immanent according to the plateau of 3rd of September, 1939 and the king's speech. Groups in the three strata listed above would have been affected differently by the complete cycle of the 'tobacco death-wish', yet the immanent-affect of smoking at the time was impossible to entirely escape, unless one was perhaps a hermit or lived in an extremely remote community. Furthermore, a generation of children were unknowingly turned into smokers by passive means, as the homes they grew up in were already filled with tobacco smoke. As has been latterly understood, analysed and recorded, passive smoking can be as lethal as the actual act of smoking, and the plateau of the 3rd of September, 1939, acts like 'spongy-substance' in terms of absorbing and spreading the 'tobacco death-wish'. In effect, there is a miasmic haze associated with the 'tobacco death-wish' that makes clear vision difficult and wafts across differences, boundaries and divisions, as we look back in order to understand the social history of the plateau. One of the most relevant and important aspects of the social history of this chapter and the underbelly of the plateau of the 3rd of September, 1939, is framing what life was like for the majority of the population at the time.

Living in the miasma

One could be forgiven for having a romanticised and exaggerated idea of the position of the British 'working or lower' classes in the plateau of the 3rd of September, 1939. For example, in my family, the myth and narrative of the 'chirpy cockney' still exists and adds a certain subjective weight to speaking about what it was like to live in pre-war London. The 'chirpy cockney' is resourceful, intelligent, fast with language, optimistically works 'against the odds', a survivor, and able to negotiate the world of street markets, tenements, the docks, cockney slang, pubs and crime. Given these formidable character traits, going to war and the king's speech might have seemed like minor incumbencies compared to the animated and interactive worldview of the 'chirpy cockney'. Yet this was far from the truth, the Second World War was a death sentence for hundreds of thousands of 'chirpy cockneys', both in Europe, the rest of the world, and in their East End of London tenements which were repeatedly bombed. The tobacco miasma floats in front of and through the subjectivity involved with living in the East End of London before the Second World War, making the evaluation of the quality of life confusing and contradictory. The facts are that coming from the East End made formal education inaccessible and upward social mobility was limited, because possessing the cockney accent was a marker to being part of an underclass, who were restricted and shunned from the halls of power. Pre-war cockneys were very fast at talking, but could barely read or write.

Most of the historical records that we have about living through the plateau of the 3rd of September, 1939, come from the perspectives of the two strata that existed on top of and parallel to the 'working or lower' classes, but are still articulated through the miasma.

I can write these words because I received a free comprehensive education in the 1970s and 1980s, went to study at university and now work as a lecturer in a university in Australia. My father was considered lucky to have been ushered into the folds of the National Union of Printing, Bookbinding and Paper Workers (NUPBPW) via an apprenticeship and an introduction by his father, but received no formal education or any further work choices other than becoming a printer. He was too young to serve in the Second World War, but was conscripted to participate in the Cypriot conflict in the 1950s, where he received a serious head injury that has permanently restricted his linguistic abilities. Both of my father's parents died from lung cancer. I have asked him what life was like in pre-war London, he was a boy at the time and has memories of the East End of London context, where he lived with his parents, two sisters and grandmother in a terraced house. The identity formation of being a 'chirpy cockney' has deeply marked my father, and still determines the ways in which he speaks about life in the miasma. He perhaps very wisely chose not to smoke, because of the early death of his father from lung cancer in the 1950s, and the association of smoking with heavy drinking, which he has also consciously avoided. My father is able to see through the miasma to a certain extent because as a boy he was evacuated during the Second World War to a semi-rural location where children were taken to escape the wartime bombing. In his retirement, he has returned to this rural life, away from the miasma and the 'tobacco death-wish'. The point here is that oral accounts of social life on the bottom rung of society during the period of the 3rd of August, 1939, have the potential to authentically tell us something about 'living in the miasma'. The miasma restricts clear sight and makes deep breathing difficult, yet at the same time, the miasma strangely enhances subjectivity, as it creates an interconnected tobacco-filled, immanent plane of interaction.

My father escaped the direct physical effects of 'living in the miasma' by not smoking and moving to the countryside. Yet he still wishes to recreate the experience of being a working class cockney by going to dancehall type events, where they celebrate in the style of the song: 'Knees Up Mother Brown'. Therefore, his memories and thoughts still work through and enact the orally gifted 'chirpy cockney' character, that was impressed into and onto him by 'living in the miasma'. The effects of the poisonous cloud of tobacco smoke, contained in the very substance of the 3rd of September, 1939, can still make its way through such memories and recreation, even though no cigarettes are consumed. In effect, at these ersatz pre-war, working class events, subjectivity is enhanced and augmented, consciousness is altered, and participants experience a type of proxy 'tobacco-high'. This is one of the reasons why there is still an extraordinary nostalgia for this pre-war period, despite the obvious problems of living at the time such as poverty, joblessness, crime and a lack of access to formal education or healthcare. 'Living in the miasma' includes a form of enhanced consciousness associated with the communal effects of smoking tobacco. Such enhancement blurs and obscures the difficulties of 'living in the miasma', and makes rebellion against such living conditions virtually inconceivable. For example, the character of the 'chirpy cockney' includes a conformity to and conditioning by the effects of 'living in the miasma' and the 'tobacco death-wish' that consequently made acceptance of the tenets of the king's speech likely, and reactionary, right-wing opinions possible. The augmentation of consciousness by living in the interconnected, addictive and immanent miasma of tobacco smoke excluded pacifism or the thought of conscientious objection to the war, and made a necessity of a palpable and well defined 'other'. This 'other' was primarily the bogey-man, Adolf Hitler (see below and chapter 5), who acted as a focus for the repressions of life in the miasma, and the violence of the 'tobacco death-wish'. Firstly, it is worth exploring what pacifism and conscientious objection add with respect to the immanence of the plateau of the 3rd of September, 1939.

Pacifism and conscientious objection

My father decided not to smoke, yet fought in the British army in the Cypriot conflict of the 1950s and was seriously injured. My grandfather, his father, who was an adult during the height of the tobacco miasma, was a heavy smoker, even growing tobacco in his tiny backyard in the East End of London, and he subsequently died in the 1950s of lung cancer. My grandfather was a conscientious objector during the Second World War. This brief and incomplete oral history of an example of life in the miasma, demonstrates some of the contradictions and complexities of thinking about the plateau of the 3rd of September, 1939. My father's father had become politicised during the 1930s as a member of the National Union of Printing, Bookbinding and Paper Workers in London (*the Times* Chapel), and had, legend has it, fought on the streets against the right wing fascists of Oswald Mosley, including the famous 'Battle of Cable Street' in 1936. Yet my father will not discuss what happened to his father during the Second World War, despite my insistent requests. This is an example of what the 'chirpy cockney' persona, raised in the miasma, will not enunciate. As a conscientious objector, one was part of a misunderstood minority of the population, who risked being sent to prison for the duration of the conflict and was often socially vilified and ostracised as a coward.

According to official records, in World War II, following the National Service (Armed Forces) Act of 1939, that was passed on the 3rd of September, 1939, there were nearly 61,000 registered conscientious objectors in the UK. Testing by Conscientious

Objection Tribunals, that had previously been set up during World War I, begun after the 3rd of September 1939, but this time they were chaired by a judge, and were much less severe than twenty years before. For example, if one was not attached to the Quakers or a similar pacifist church, it was considered adequate to prove conscientious objection by stating that you disagreed with: "warfare as a means of settling international disputes," a line from the Kellogg-Briand Pact of 1928. The tribunals granted full exemption, exemption depending on alternative service, exemption only from fighting duties, or dismissal of the submission. Of the 61,000 who applied for conscientious objection status, only 3,000 were given complete exemption and 18,000 were defined as false claims. Of those ordered to do non-combatant military service, almost 7000 were allocated to the Non-Combatant Corps (NCC), set up in mid-1940, its companies functioned in clothing and food shops, in transport, or in any military project not requiring the handling of "material of an aggressive nature". In November 1940, it was decided to grant troops in the NCC to work in bomb disposal[29]. In total over 350 volunteered. Other non-combatants were drafted into the Royal Army Medical Corps. Other acceptable jobs were farm work, mining, fire-fighting and the ambulance service. About 5500 objectors were imprisoned and charged with offences relating to their unrecognised objection. A further 1000 were court-martialled by the armed forces and sent to military detention barracks or civil prisons. Nevertheless, the stigma attached to 'conchies' (as conscientious objectors were called) was tremendous, regardless of the genuineness of their motives and cowardice was often imputed.

I do not know what happened to my grandfather during World War II amongst the 61,000 conscientious objectors. I know that he was of 'fighting age', i.e. he was between the ages of 18-41 on the 3rd of September 1939, and that he was a conscientious objector, though I do not know if exemption was granted to him, if he worked in some capacity to help with the war effort, or if he was jailed. Many communists went to fight against the fascists in Europe and beyond, yet he was not one of them. I know that he did not hold strong religious beliefs, and that he was not a Quaker. The miasma covers up this period of his life like a poison gas attack. It is clear that he was affected by the 'tobacco death-wish', due to his heavy smoking and subsequent death from lung cancer, yet the raised and connected consciousness of life in the miasma obscures his contribution or otherwise to the war effort. As I sit and wonder what happened to him, from a different perspective and stratum as discussed above, which has been raised out of the miasma by the effects of the free British comprehensive education and the healthcare war on smoking, I can't help but express the desire to reconcile my grandfather as a pacifist. The movement of pacifism could be included under an umbrella of left-leaning social movements, similar to Gandhi's non-violent political movement, which eventually helped to topple Britain's rule of India. Pacifists would have directly objected to the war on the grounds of the inevitable violence and death that was required to square up militarily to the rise of 'Nazi Germany'. The more complex issue for the plateau of September the 3rd, 1939, concerns the position of pacifists with respect to capitalism. As mentioned above, many communists fought on the side of the allies and against fascism, due to the barbarity of the Nazi regime with respect to, for example, anti-Semitism. Yet that act also meant fighting against the anti-capitalism of Hitler's 'National Socialists', and on the side of, for example, those who controlled the global tobacco trade. The point here is not to artificially glorify my heritage, or to create an unnecessary mythology around one person, but to fully under-stand the political-social-cultural issues that run through the plateau of the 3rd of September, 1939, and that are relevant today to a 'capitalised education'.

Mahatma Gandhi the pacifist received similar ridicule in the press as did Hitler, the anti-Semite monster in 1939. Both figures were 'othered' through the miasma at the time — one as the enemy of civilization, democracy, human rights (Hitler); the other due to the alternative and mystical nature of the path of absolute non-violence (Gandhi). Clearly, both positions were open to attack from a nationalistic, British Commonwealth perspective, yet the pacifism of Gandhi and possibly my grandfather, is arguably the most troublesome with respect to the immanent materialism of this book and the eventual 'capitalised education' which we see now with KM as media object. When Britain was on the brink of full-scale, deadly war on the 3rd of September, 1939, a breakout of widespread pacifism amongst the British working classes would have been terrifying for the ruling political and social elites. The collective and loosely connected hippie movements of the late 1960s and 1970s in the USA and beyond were 'anti-war', and could perhaps be seen to have taken over the mantle of Gandhi and non-violent rebellion. Yet the non-violent rebellions of the 1960s and 1970s have also been latterly dealt with by the forces of capitalism[30], for example, the original 1970s celebratory free festivals have been almost entirely commercialised, e.g. the Glastonbury celebration in west England, because messages or arguments of opposition to living a mainstream capitalised working lifestyle have been systematically ridiculed, repressed or shut down by the conditions and ethics of working life outside of the festivities[31]. The time that my grandfather, the potential pacifist, spent during the Second World War, has been eradicated from my family's collective memory, because concentrated non-action is an anathema to participating in capitalist and work-based society. Life in the miasma, however murky, included positive action, whether for or against the prevailing winds of capitalism. The political alternatives to capitalism or communism and fascism shall be explored in more depth in chapter 5. Here it is worth dwelling on the important creation of 'the other' through the miasma of this plateau, which I will call after the common myth, 'The Bogey Man'.

The Bogey Man

The miasma of the tobacco haze created by the plateau of the 3rd of September, 1939, makes clear vision difficult and monsters are easy to create in the gloom. King George the VI doesn't mention Hitler or 'The Bogey Man' in his speech, yet refers to an unspecified other who uses military force without restraint and against 'us'. This unspecified other was solidified and emboldened in the contemporary British press and became a definite other through the real figure of Adolf Hitler. Adolf Hitler was an ideal 'Bogey Man' in that he could take on monstrous proportions whilst delivering fluent oratory performances in front of impassioned audiences. However, the Bogey Man is by its nature mutative and hybrid, and can take over different persona as well as settle onto ideal types such as Adolf Hitler. As mentioned above, Mahatma Gandhi was another pivotal Bogey Man for the plateau of the 3rd of September, 1939, and was in many ways a more complex figure to demonize due to his chosen path of non-violent resistance to British colonial rule. Yet both Hitler and Gandhi are joined in their interchangeable 'Bogey Man' status in terms of articulation, as expressed by Donna Haraway:

> Articulation is not a simple matter. Language is the effect of articulation, and so are bodies. The articulate are jointed animals; they are not smooth like the perfect spherical animals of Plato's origin fantasy in the *Timaeus*. The articulate are cobbled together[32].

Donna Haraway was primarily concerned with the images of nature and women as others and their relationships with language and scientific knowledge. In this immanent materialist study, the effects of using language are considerable in terms of the miasmic creation of monsters. The identified monsters on the

3rd of September, 1939, of Hitler and Gandhi were both highly articulate, and that functionality augmented their status beyond the miasmic tobacco smoke, where it was often difficult to tell who was speaking, or how one could align words with subjectivity and meaning. The miasmic blur caused an inward yet strong dimension to exist in the plane of the 3rd of September, 1939, which tends to augment subjective traits, characterises, for example by the 'chirpy cockney', but does not have a coherent political message. The 'chirpy cockney' may be able to speak very quickly and adapt to difficult living conditions, yet this flux-like and mutable character is not attached to any one political perspective, but floats between political identities, and attaches to issues connected as racism, economics, population, immigration, nationalism, violence and sexism in a reactive manner. The Bogey Man is a form of pre-rational monster meant to scare children into obeying societal rules, and in the case of the 'chirpy cockney' living in the miasma, the Bogey Man was a figure of subjective articulation and extra-rational language use. In contrast to being able to cleverly react and adapt to changing environmental factors, the Bogey Men of Hitler and Gandhi were able to recreate the world through language and to some extent appear to direct the life around them.

Living in the miasma made such articulation nearly impossible. The king's speech wafted through the cloud smoke and over the radio waves in an educated, refined, delicate and aesthetic manner. The king was not a Bogey Man for the British, even though much of the historic and continued domination of the social order by the aristocracy depended on the violent repression of rebellion against any challenges to the pre-established class system. The disadvantaged populations living in the miasma were unconsciously controlled by setting up and maintaining the influence of the 'Bogey Man' in the forms of Hitler and Gandhi in the mainstream of British life. The 'Bogey Man' manifested many of the issues that characters such as the 'chirpy cockney' reacted against, therefore taking away the potency of rebellion against the established aristocratic order. Of course, such a simplistic psychological narrative is not wholly the case, as the immanent plane of becoming through and around the 3rd of September, 1939 was complex enough for one to make different choices to the stark ones of obedience or non-obedience to the king's speech, e.g. non-violent civil disobedience. What is interesting in terms of our retrospective view of the plateau is that the 'chirpy cockneys' were in the main conscripted and went to war to fight against the 'Bogey Man' and their forces. As discussed above, the most revolutionary position of the time was, arguably, pacifism and the subjectivity of the conscientious objector. In contrast, the majority of communists in Britain went to fight against Hitler because of the monstrous nature of the Nazi regime, demonstrated in, for example, anti-Semitism. This statement leads us to question the ways in which the figure of the 'Bogey Man' potentially masked the capitalist and anti-capitalist intentions of war.

Capitalism and Anti-capitalism

Capitalism in this chapter has been characterised by the example of the tobacco trade. The thesis of this chapter is that the immanent materialism of the tobacco trade spreads out and consumes other activities, communities, subjectivity and all cultural production through the functioning of the plateau of the 3rd of September, 1939. Smoking tobacco is highly addictive, so it is a superb capitalist product, its usage creating needs in the user of an unconscious, physiological and internal nature. Furthermore, the miasma of the tobacco smoke creates a host of related effects, interconnections and ways of doing things that make differences from the 'tobacco norm' hard to imagine or initiate. The tobacco trade depends on international treaties being upheld and honoured between producers and buyers in different countries, and interlinked and synchronous lines of:

tobacco planting, growing, harvesting, drying, transportation, manufacture, distribution, marketing, sales, consumption and monetary exchange. All of these thoroughly connected aspects of the tobacco trade produce jobs, revenue and a mode of life for those involved, and these modes can be established all over the world. One can therefore see that there is a political way of thinking about and defending the tobacco trade, similar in kind to the ways in which the mining trade has been conceived of and defended more recently. In short, there can be no doubt that the decision to go to war on the 3rd of September, 1939, was in part to defend the international system of capitalism against the wholesale challenges to the status quo as manifested by fascism and communism (see chapter 5).

The philosophical stance of immanent materialism of this book does not determine one's positioning in terms of capitalism or anti-capitalism. Rather, one constructs a plateau in order to understand the immanent flows of material that were impacting on life at the time. These flows are pre-personal, chaotic, inter-related and vital. Much of one's comprehension of the flows could be rendered through determining the stage of techno-logical development that the plateau represents, as was seen through the digitalisation of cyborg capitalism in chapter 1. In and about the plateau of the 3rd of September, 1939, the major technological drivers of both capitalism and anti-capitalism were the continued use of coal as a major energy source and the rapidly emerging use of oil as coal's heir apparent. The decla-ration of war by King George VI in his speech could be read as a geopolitical statement, meant to solidify Britain's claim on the remaining Commonwealth territories, the trade routes and in particular, the flows of coal and oil. The downgrading of the British Empire to the looser title of the British Commonwealth in the speech was a loss in terms of the symbolic power base of the British from its height (see chapter 3) and this change became irreversible after India and Pakistan gained independence in

1947. However, the influence of the British Commonwealth in world affairs was still extensive in 1939, including holding territories in every continent on Earth. These territories could only be reached and governed by ship, train, truck, aeroplane, motor car and radio, and these technologies acted as the arteries and infrastructure for international capitalism from a British perspective. One might lament with respect to the palpable and physical nature of capitalism at the time, as the extensive financialisation through cybernetic networks of world trade that we see today had not taken place (see chapter 7); however, it was this physical infrastructure of capitalism from a British perspective that was under threat due to war, and this defines an aspect of immanence of the plane.

The Bogey Man focuses, humanises and in an augmented way, demonises the immanence of the threat to world capitalist infrastructure. The gloomy tobacco miasma helps to create tension and atmosphere with respect to the Bogey Man, and this dramatisation of the plane makes the truth of infrastructural protection immanent. If one could go back in time and track the flows of coal and oil around the globe on the 3rd of September, 1939, one would be able to notice the ways in which this vital infrastructure was strategically protected by pro-capitalist forces and under attack from those pertaining to anti-capitalism. The nationalistic, imperial game of territorial colonialisation (see chapter 3) had been replaced by a politicised world of intrigue and espionage around strategic infrastructure. One of the most interesting aspects of the plane of the 3rd of September, 1939, was the potential for spying and identity recreation, as capitalist and anti-capitalist forces were at war on the ideological and psychological fronts as well as on the actual battlefield. For example, an English speaking German with knowledge of chemical engineering and loyal to the Nazi Party, could try to infiltrate a British fuel company and ascertain information about, for example, the oilfields of Persia and the relevant oilfield supply routes. There is an aspect of an identity double, and doubling identity effects with respect to the plane of the 3rd of September, 1939, as the widespread and vital protection of infrastructure became politicised through the global clashing of capitalist and anti-capitalist forces.

The doubling of identities brings to mind the stylised films of the period. For example, one could say that *Casablanca* the Warner Brothers' wartime romantic thriller, includes the immanent doubling of identities through its depictions of character, location, plot and action. The main plot of the film revolves around obtaining free passes to travel through Nazi Germany controlled Europe to neutral Portugal, and these passes had come into the hands of a cynical yet resourceful American nightclub owner called Rick, played by Humphrey Bogart. Dramatic tension is maintained throughout the film by the disguised, transitory and double-sided characters and plot-twists, even though the script does also rely on multiple clichés as suggested by Umberto Eco[33]. The location is pivotal to the augmentation of the doubling effects in the film, as control of North Africa was of vital strategic importance in terms of access to the Mediterranean and the Suez Canal at its southeastern tip. William Burroughs latterly called this part of North Africa 'the interzone'[34], because of the ways in which characters there blended and doubled, and many edged subjectivities were the norm. There is immanence in the interzone, which is depicted through the atmosphere and tension of the film, and comes from the ways in which capitalist and anti-capitalist forces were jostling for control of the lines of power that ran through this North African portal to world trade. The film suggests an underlying conflict in nationalism rather than capitalism and anti-capitalism, for example, when the band at Rick's place start playing 'la Marseillaise', yet the clearly pro-capitalist perspective of this American film, could not associate the French resistance with left-wing politics. Rather, the lines of difference drawn from national characteristics better framed the

American film viewers' expectations and desires, in contrast to, for example, questioning the film's capitalist message. The use of this 1942 film to illustrate aspects of the immanence of the plateau of the 3rd of September, 1939, highlights the visual impact of the plane and the ways in which time could be called into question through particular forms of cinematic visualisation[35].

Time and visualisation

When one speaks about the effect of doubling in character traits, the Bogey Man and the miasma with respect to the plane of immanence of the 3rd of September, 1939, what are we talking about? Certainly one is referencing aspects of memory, in contrast to, for example chapter 6 of this book, which constructs the plane of immanence of 1150-1200, and is therefore primarily a historical reconstruction, even though elements of the plateau of 1150-1200 are still apparent in the formation of the 'capitalised education' of Kate Middleton and in chapter 7, e.g., the romanticism of the plane. The fact that we have universally recognised filmic depictions of the synthetic elements of the plane of the 3rd of September, 1939, as depicted by *Casablanca*, and that direct relatives such as my father were alive on the 3rd of September, 1939, means that the plane is not wholly constructed from reconstructed historical elements. In a similar manner to the plane of the 31st of August, 1997 (chapter 1) and the 29th of April, 2011 (chapter 7), the ways in which immanence works with respect to the plateau also relies on memory, recognition and the visual aspects of thought, e.g. projection. One could say that by watching *Casablanca*, the original black-and-white version, or by going through my father's collection of old black-and-white photographs of family life in the East End of London before the Second World War, one is visually engaging with the immanence of the plane. This is because the effect of character doubling, the Bogey Man and the miasma are parallel and layered elements, which are actively inter-related in the act of visualisation. Time is stretched and synthesised by watching the film or by rifling through the old photographs, and this experience is mixed up with dreams, identity, memories, hopes and desires. This is why the plane of immanence of the 3rd of September, 1939, seems to aggrandise and attract sentimental nostalgia into its orbit, even though it was in reality a dark and prophetic day of foreboding.

Perhaps the best example of this point comes in the recent film of 'The King's Speech'. In the film, the subjectivity of the king is explored alongside his relationship with the speech therapist, Lionel Logue. The king comes across as being a victim of circumstance, dominated by the speech defect, and unable to break free of the social humiliation that this defect has bestowed on his life. This effect of the film is enhanced by one's own reaction to the persona of the king, and how one might cope with the reality of having a serious speech defect in a role that required clear and unambiguous speech. There is a powerful inward motion working here, perhaps one can simultaneously remember a time when one was humiliated in public, or felt ashamed at something one has said. The 'affect' of watching the film runs through us in the ways in which one begins to build a sympathetic and empathetic relationship with the king by viewing the film, even if one remembers that he was still in fact an imperial ruler of a vast empire, largely governed by military force. The experience of watching the film takes us into the immanence of the plane of the 3rd of September, 1939, and the projection of the king as a real person, with all his frailties and flaws. In truth, if we came from either of the first two strata as listed in the first section of this chapter above, the king would have been an extremely remote figure, living in a different world of privilege, riches and luxury. The visual projection of the king in the film is therefore a false one that masks over the power base upon which he ruled.

It is in the act of projection that time is elongated and thoughts intermingle with memories, dreams, hopes, identities and desires. Perhaps one could see oneself in the shoes of Lionel Logue, a largely self-taught speech therapist from Australia, contracted to treat one of the most powerful men in the world. The effect of watching the film is to imagine oneself as larger, to aggrandise and to return to the pre-war period with sentimental nostalgia for the 'way things used to be'. The aggrandising and nostalgic effect of the plateau of September the 3rd, 1939, works in contrast to the next chapter 3, which constructs the plateau of 1877, and the declaration of the British Empire. Certainly, there was enormous aggrandisement in 1877, but it comes without the nostalgia, the sentiment is different as shall be seen. Hidden between the lines of the king's speech of the 3rd of September, 1939, there is a yearning for the way things were in 1877, when the British ruled over an empire, when the monarch didn't have a speech impediment in public, when the British didn't have to fight against the forces of anti-capitalism, and when the aristocracy still had an unassailable grip on power. Furthermore, one is subjectively located through the immanence of the plane of the 3rd of September, 1939, in a contrasting way to 1877, because the identity doubling effect, Bogey Man and miasma play on the expectations and thoughts one might have about actually living through the period. When I try to visualise myself living in an East End of London tenement and listening to the king's speech on the 3rd of September, 1939, I am affected by the recent film version of the event, by my father's account of the period, by my father's memory of his father—the pacifist, in my mind—and by Humphrey Bogart. It is especially tempting to frame the plateau through Bogart's character in *Casablanca*, as he was able to project a sense of inimical freedom with respect to the double-crosses, intrigues, conspiracy and espionage around him. It would be impossible to identify a similar character with respect to the plateau of 1877.

The plateau of September 3rd, 1939, has a strongly visual quality, which is enhanced and synthesised through the ways in which this period has been represented in film, literature (e.g. the novel *1984*) and documentaries about the lead up to World War II. This powerful visual quality plays with the linear nature of time and makes contemplation of the plane a form of internalisation connected to identity doubles, Bogey Men and the miasma. The upwardly mobile aspect of the plane of 1939 came after the Second World War, when a Labour government was returned in the United Kingdom, largely through the wishes of the battle-weary returning soldiers, and improvements in free healthcare and education began in earnest and disqualified the question: Whose Education? The aristocracy and their feudal system of domestic service in Britain suffered hugely in this post-war period through the crippling inheritance tax, which left many families unable to maintain their estates. The 3rd of September, 1939, took place before these widespread changes in education, health and domestic service to the aristocracy had happened, it also transpired before waves of post-war immigrants arrived in the United Kingdom. For example, my parents and their families lived in the East End of London, as I have mentioned above. These areas have been latterly 'taken over' in their eyes by the post-war immigrants, who have largely come from ex-British Empire colonies such as India, Pakistan and the West Indies. The point here is not to side with the anti-immigration stance that some East Enders have taken, but to understand how the immanence of the 3rd of September, 1939 functions. More specifically, the immanent nostalgia for the plane of the king's speech is a form of internalisation and longing for a time before post-war immigration, educational equality, the freedom from servitude and universal healthcare. One could say that the 'chirpy cockney' had to be quick and to take his or her chances before the war, as they were likely to be fleeting moments of opportunity through the miasmic haze.

Conclusion

The powerful collection of intensities that have been described in this chapter, still affect us, as we interact with KM as media object in the 21st century. This is because of the nostalgic and nationalistic set of emotions that are attached to this plateau. Unlike chapters 1 and 7, the most recent dates in this story about KM as media object and a capitalised education, the sense of this chapter, timed just before the Second World War, is of past glories, and the last dying days of the British Empire. In contrast, chapters 1 and 7 evoke a bland sense of the familiar, the usual and normality under the 'capitalist real'. The plateau of September the 3rd, 1939 has disappeared, despite the right-wing advertising campaigns of the UK Conservative Party, or the Queen's best wishes to keep the memory of her dead father alive. However, the introduction of broadcasting by George VI for and on the international stage, and the consequences of World War II, such as the National Health Service and a comprehensive education system are still with us. The immanent projection and use of KM as media object can clearly be traced through to the plateau of this chapter, with the intervening date of August the 31st, 1997, and the death of Diana Spencer, also figuring in the equation. However, to fully understand the immanent materialism of this chapter, one has to link it with the next plateau of 1877 and the declaration of the British Empire.

Chapter 3

The declaration of Empire and a climate of fear:

Queen Victoria/Disraeli—1877

Introduction

62 years before the king's speech of the 3rd of September, 1939, Queen Victoria had been declared the Empress of India by her then prime minister, Benjamin Disraeli. The year of 1877 was from the British perspective a momentous one, which saw the British colonies around the world collectively referred to as an 'empire' for the first time. This chapter will construct the plateau of the year 1877 from an immanent materialist philosophical perspective by extracting the most relevant and motive elements from this date in order to constitute the plane of immanence of 1877. Unlike the first two chapters of this book and chapter 7, the immanence of 1877 does not work due to memory or relayed memory, as we cannot extract first-hand accounts of what life was like in 1877 from anybody living today. Yet one should not be daunted by the notion of historical reconstruction, as many of the recorded, historical elements of 1877 are still powerful and immanent today, and these factors are cognisant with respect to the 'capitalised education' of Kate Middleton. The primary danger of the historical reconstruction of the plane of immanence of 1877 is the misunderstanding and misplacement of subjective forces into the plane as synthetic objects that could henceforth populate the plane and lend it consistency and weight. For example, the use of the adjective 'momentous' above with respect to the British Empire could be misinterpreted as pride, aggran-disement—as discussed in chapter 2 from a different perspective—or superiority, and result in a lofted, transcendent

perspective for this chapter. Of course, this is exactly what we are attempting to avoid through the deliberate injection of immanent materialism into the frame, and throughout the book, even when discussing perhaps the zenith of British rule and dominion. One cannot forget that the British Empire was simultaneously built on violence, racism, technological advantage, unfair trade deals, slavery and elitism, as well as the ingenuity and good fortune of the British nation. At the same time that Queen Victoria was being declared Empress by Benjamin Disraeli, Karl Marx was clinically analysing and writing about the system of capitalism on which the British Empire was predicated, and therefore his work forms a pivotal underbelly to the 'transport' of empire talk and imagery.

To construct the plane of immanence of 1877, we need to get our 'hands dirty', and understand what the other side of empire success was like. The patriotic Union Jack flag waving, the vast symbolic ceremony, the tremendous use of ritualised event and the association of empire with civilization, godliness and 'the right' was in part an elaborate diversion to hide the reality of life in the slums, and the lack of education and healthcare for most of the lower and working classes at the time. The three tier class system that we saw in the immanence of the last chapter was absolute in 1877, and the feudal servant system of the aristocracy was an immutable part of many peoples' lives. If one was born a servant, one was likely to die a servant, and life was constituted by innumerable tasks directed to the wellbeing and maintenance of the aristocracy. Incredibly, many of these systems of domestic service are still operating today in terms of the lives of the British royal family and several of the most powerful aristocratic families, who have been able to survive the post-war inheritance tax and the increasing household bills of the last 135 years. Likewise, the capitalist system of 1877 as promulgated by the British has since mutated and has been accelerated since the year of this plateau (see chapters 1, 2 and 7), but has survived, and is

now considered by some to be the 'only game in town'. To understand how and why this has happened, one needs to construct
the Queen Victoria/Disraeli plateau of 1877, this includes the
naming of the British Empire, and the realisation of the conditions through which the empire could henceforth prosper.

British idealism

The tradition of British idealism has been largely discarded in
intellectual circles today, due to, in part, the criticisms of Bertrand
Russell and G.E. Moore, and the supersession of idealism in
Britain by the materialism of analytic philosophy[36]. Yet in 1877,
the tradition was still alive, theorised and practised by advocates
such as Thomas Hill Green. What is interesting from the
perspective of immanent materialism and this book is that British
idealism was an intellectual attempt to 'theorise the whole', and
this included all political and practical forms of life, functioning
in the plateau of 1877. In contrast, one could argue that analytic
philosophy has latterly become reductively tied to questions that
principally concern language and logic. Thomas Hill Green
advocated self-realisation in all things[37], and this approach influenced educational philosophers, such as the American John
Dewey, who theorised learning in terms of the development of
the self or constructivism. One could say that in the immanent
materialist analysis of this chapter, the empire material conditions of domination and power were buoyed, and in a reciprocal
feedback relationship of aggrandisement with respect to British
idealism. This was an age of civil activism in Britain, and this
activism included: the establishment of a multiplicity of civil
regulations and laws; the expansion of local and provincial
councils and governance at all levels of society; the proliferation
of clubs with their requisite memberships and membership
requirements; and the development of charities, philanthropy
and workhouses. In contrast to German idealism, as theorised
primarily by Hegel, the self-realisation of Thomas Hill Green did

not aggregate into the formulation of an over-arching rational state system that controlled particular self-realisation projects. The idealism of Hill was 'granulised' in terms of the particular civic societies and schemes for improvement, whereas Hegelian idealism projected a homogeneous uplifting in general and in step with the functioning of the state, 'the dialectic' and *aufhebung*[38].

The contrast between British idealism and German idealism indicates an important aspect of the immanence of the plane of 1877. The point here is not whether or not Hegel or Hill were 'right', but how these philosophies were reflected in the overall systems of life that were apparent at the time. Both Britain and Germany were locked in battle in 1877 for colonial domination of the world, yet the British had gained the ascendency in terms of secure international shipping routes and the provision of an empire via these secured routes. Vital to these trade routes was an efficient and well-organised bureaucracy that kept the colonial outposts supplied and regulated and an effective military presence on the ground if anything went wrong in operations or if there was a rebellion. The power of the British Empire in 1877 was not stable or in a state of equilibrium, but was synchronised with the establishment of global capitalism and with private enterprise, which was encouraged and controlled through the system of bureaucracy in London that was called 'the civil service'. The British had engineered profit from their colonial territories through companies such as the East India Company, and had made great use of the leverage which such companies had given them in local areas around the world. It is in the myriad and potentially mutually beneficial relationships between state and private ingenuity, that the immanence of the British system may be located. In other words, the capital flows of the state are not absolute or sanctioned off in the British Empire. One is led to believe that one may gain access to the riches of the empire through adventure, good fortune, calculation, hard work and innovation. In reality, the immanence of the British Empire was controlled and regulated by the class system, property rights, tax, the rules of the civil service and forms of industrial ownership that Marx theorised whilst he lived in London, i.e. the control of the means to production.

Marx perceived a way out of capitalism precisely through an extension and retheorisation of Hegel's philosophy, but without the idealism. Marx came up with the notion of the 'material dialectic', which was a means to understand how the lower and working classes were in a state of constant agitation and potential revolt with respect to the clearly unfair living conditions that were apparent at the birth of the British Empire. The immanence of the situation came about, according to Marx, precisely because to the nature of capital, and because there must be constant exchange for capitalism to work, i.e. capital constantly comes up against an internal barrier with respect to itself[39]. Because capital is calculated as a physical quantity, which was dominated in 1877 by the extraordinary international exchange value of the Pound Sterling, it was impossible to distribute wealth and capital at a fast enough rate for real exchange to work. Marx predicted that the state must inevitably take over the means to production through socialism, because the reliance on private enterprise would result in vast and irresolvable inequalities between the rich and the poor, and that total class war between industrialists and workers would eventually take place. The takeover of industrial production happened as Marx predicted, and as we shall see in chapter 5 in Russia and Germany, where anti-capitalist forces gained the ascendency in the early nineteenth century. However, Marx could not have predicted the rise of the new digital technologies that have hugely aided the ways in which the system of capitalism has been able to mutate and sustain itself, and ultimately develop to a position that some might argue is now virtually unassailable (see chapter 7). I would contend that part of the reason that capitalism has become so all-encompassing is due to the specific immanence of 1877 and the plateau of Queen Victoria/Disraeli at the birth of the empire. Such immanence was not entirely due to class struggle or the immanent nature of capital as Marx suggested[40]. The particular type of British idealism that existed in 1877 has resulted in an enduring mode of conservatism that is suspicious and antagonistic to any form of anti-capitalist or revolutionary action, and is indeed immanent through 'capitalist life'. The form of British idealism of 1877 is allied with Christianity, anti-statism, general calls for personal freedom, and the militarisation and protection of capitalism.

"Onward, Christian Soldiers"

One could be forgiven for underestimating the power of Christianity in 1877, as we retrospectively construct the plateau of that year from its then future. However the immanence of the plane undoubtedly includes: the fastidious and zealous work of the Christian missionaries throughout the British Empire, Disraeli and Queen Victoria's particular angles and projections of the Anglican faith, and the implacable yet mobile relationships between the philosophical work of the British idealists such as Thomas Hill Green, a general belief in God, and the practice of the accompanying Christian metaphysics in universities and schools in Britain. The theme song for such immanence is the hymn, "Onward, Christian Soldiers", which was composed during this period:

1. Onward, Christian soldiers, marching as to war,
with the cross of Jesus going on before.
Christ, the royal Master, leads against the foe;
forward into battle see his banners go!

Refrain:

Onward, Christian soldiers, marching as to war,

with the cross of Jesus going on before.

2. At the sign of triumph Satan's host doth flee;
on then, Christian soldiers, on to victory!
Hell's foundations quiver at the shout of praise;
brothers, lift your voices, loud your anthems raise.
(Refrain)

3. Like a mighty army moves the church of God;
brothers, we are treading where the saints have trod.
We are not divided, all one body we,
one in hope and doctrine, one in charity.
(Refrain)

4. Crowns and thrones may perish, kingdoms rise and wane,
but the church of Jesus constant will remain.
Gates of hell can never 'gainst that church prevail;
we have Christ's own promise, and that cannot fail.
(Refrain)

5. Onward then, ye people, join our happy throng,
blend with ours your voices in the triumph song.
Glory, laud, and honour unto Christ the King,
this through countless ages men and angels sing.
(Refrain)

Perhaps one of the most confusing aspects of such immanence in 1877 is that it was dressed up as transcendence. Even when rereading the words of the hymn above today, one can imagine and recreate the refrain of this song delivered with gusto in provisional Anglican churches, one can sense the tone of the voices and feel the ways in which the song makes the singers come together, one can understand how the congregation may be invigorated and impassioned into an 'army'. These effects of the hymn were part of the necessary conditions for empire, and therefore immanent to the plane of 1877. This statement means that the ways in which the hymn became popularised, spread out and was taken up in widespread empire outposts, made the connections between nodes in the empire stronger, and this effect created resonance within the combined subjectivities of those charged with 'empire work'. On one level, the immanence of "Onward, Christian Soldiers" turns every harmless adminis-trator, civil servant and trader in the British Empire into a potential warrior, fighting for the idea of one world under a Christian God. On another level, the hymn helps to create homogenisation, community and unity where there quite likely had been none. The effects of enunciating hymns such as "Onward, Christian Soldiers" in a group are motivational and affective, in terms of creating one 'cause' and 'goal' for action, the spiritual curiosity of the singers may have been primarily dispersed, heterogeneous, animist or tending towards nature or connecting with 'the other' in terms of the population under colonisation. The effects of singing the song together in a Christian church are to disconnect the congregation with the outside world, to create an impasse with the actual conditions that were apparent, and to blur the edges of real life and any dangers associated with real life such as attack by the colonised. One can imagine a British church in India or elsewhere in 1877, with a congregation of British colonialists singing the song and creating such effects. In their minds they are praising God, and being transported into the sublime in a transcendent 'holy' moment, in reality, they are creating and recreating the immanent conditions for the functioning of the empire.

Integral to this aspect of immanence is a fear of 'the other'. The other in this instance is the non-white, the uncivilised, savages, the unchristian, the uneducated, the natives, the different and the foreign. One could say that the racism of the Victorian British Empire has become infamous and therefore easy to characterise, what is not obvious, and what is vital as we construct the immanent plane of 1877 is just how this particular form of racism functioned at the time. The statement: 'Racism was endemic' is meaningless, the point and power of the immanence of hymns such as "Onward, Christian Soldiers" is exemplified by the writings of a young Cecil Rhodes (1877):

> The idea gleaming and dancing before one's eyes like a will-of-the-wisp at last frames itself into a plan. Why should we not form a secret society with but one object the furtherance of the British Empire and the bringing of the whole uncivilised world under British rule for the making the Anglo-Saxon race but one Empire... It is our duty to seize every opportunity of acquiring more territory and we should keep this one idea steadily before our eyes that more territory simply means more of the Anglo-Saxon race, more of the best, the most human, most honourable race the world possesses... I contend that there are at the present moment numbers of the ablest men in the world who would devote their whole lives to it[41].

Please remember that Rhodes was not a madman, but a fully integrated member of the British establishment, who reflected normative views of the time. The notion of a 'secret society' that would further the cause of the British around the world was an important aspect of the immanence of the plane of 1877, and is still relevant today, but through the ways in which this notion has inverted, decayed, lacerated and fallen into disrepute. The 'secret society' was where the British Imperialists could meet and discuss their latest adventures in the colonies, where the truth of their drives that were motivating the growth of the empire could be shared, where men could enunciate what being powerful in 1877 meant in public.

Again, one should caution against becoming too enraptured with the notion of a 'secret society' as being at the heart of

Imperial expansionism. The position that Rhodes held was historical in that it was widely proposed and discussed at the time, the reality of 'secret societies' is a much more deeply embedded one, and is not particular to Rhodes or the plane of immanence of 1877. Rhodes's writing feeds off of centuries old traditions of elitism and exclusion that were manifest in the public schools of the time, and especially those of the Clarendon Commission, the continued power of the aristocracy, and the ways in which the British systems of finance, power and social influence inter-related to and depended on the public schools and the rule of the aristocracy. The point here is that these inter-locking systems were focused and accelerated by the opportunities that lay in front of them in terms of the extension and declaration of empire in 1877. One could say that 1877 was like a celestial alignment of the stars, the existing 'secret societies' of the power elite of Britain could use this alignment and step forth on it as they wished. The combined 'secret societies' of the exclusive British public schools and the aristocracy in 1877, had enormous forward energies that went back to the medieval and pre-medieval period, and as shall be analysed in chapter 6. These energies were based on the control of international capital flows, that are perhaps best understood through the ways in which early finance capitalism depended on the physical control of shipping routes, but also, the occupation of territory in terms of property laws that went back to the Norman invasion of Britain in 1066, and the ownership of industry that made products and profit from the raw materials emanating from the colonies. The 'secret societies' of Britain had an unparalleled window of expansion in 1877, but this window also depended on packs of empire workers who protected the interests of the 'secret societies'. The immanence of "Onward, Christian Soldiers" works in this way, and makes one aware of the inter-relationships between public and private religion.

The public religion of "Onward, Christian Soldiers" marks

out a collective persona of grim determination and sacrifice. The private religion of the 'secret societies' as described by Rhodes indicates a tyrannical will to power that would stop at nothing to rule the world in favour of the British. Clearly, there is a symbiotic relationship functioning here, and one that might be profitably understood through an immanent materialist analysis. The singing of hymns such as "Onward, Christian Soldiers" creates immanence through the ways in which the congregation are joined in the moment, and in that moment the singers are blinded and turned against frequently hostile empire environments; the immanence of the 'secret societies' works in reverse to hide the reality and cruelty of the empire 'probe-heads' that had to reach out across the world to expand the territories and dominion of the British. The 'secret societies' had to be acutely aware of the specific empire environments to become ensconced within new countries and to take control. One can perhaps see echoes of this immanence in the ways in which contemporary finance capitalism has to do research to understand developing and international markets (see chapter 7). The point here is that the private religion of the 'secret societies' was based on objective knowledge and a rigorous analytic examination of the situation in order to gain advantage, whereas the public religion of "Onward, Christian Soldiers" was based on the *ad hoc* transformation of individuals into packs of Christian warriors. The racism of the British Empire came from the ways in which the public and private religions worked together in 1877, and the results of such racism were felt internationally through unequal hierarchies of trade and capitalist exchange, discrimination and prejudice. These specific movements took place through the plane of immanence in 1877, whereby international monetary exchange and the subjectivities that activated exchange were personified by the ways in which "Onward, Christian Soldiers" and the 'secret societies' became combined, and this combinatory mechanism also points to particular questions about the superstructure within which such combinations could take happen.

Victorian superstructure

An emergent analysis of the ways in which the Victorian super-structure upheld global capitalism will be undertaken in chapter 4. On the plane of Queen Victoria/Disraeli in 1877, these super-structures were mature and reflexively pointed outwards in the movement of empire expansion. Marx analysed capitalist super-structure thus:

> In the social production of their existence, men inevitably enter into definite relations, which are independent of their will, namely [the] relations of production appropriate to a given stage in the development of their material forces of production. The totality of these relations of production constitutes the economic structure of society, the real foundation, on which arises a legal and political super-structure, and to which correspond definite forms of consciousness[42].

The superstructure is primarily associated with ideology, and with the ways in which a dominant culture emerges on top of and through the specific modes of economic production that were apparent at the time. The key ingredient that points to an understanding of the Victorian superstructure wherein hymns such as "Onward, Christian Soldiers" could combine success-fully with the 'secret societies' of Cecil Rhodes is the particular manipulation of Englishness and heroism at the time. On one hand, the public empire heroes of 1877 were produced on the sports fields of the Clarendon Commission schools through fair play and the love of 'manly' competition. On the other hand, one could interject that the 'real' heroes of the empire were the workers of Britain and beyond, who slaved away for their entire lives in terrible conditions to make a pittance for themselves and

enormous profits for the owners of the land, the bosses of industrial production, and the controllers of finance. Certainly, this
was the way that Marx perceived the situation in 1877, and his
dream was that this self-evident inequality would inevitably
erupt into social revolution. The immanence of Britain in 1877 is
revealed through asking the reverse question: i.e., Why did social
revolution *not* happen in Britain?

The answer to this question is a complex one, and one that
demands a detour through chapter 2 of this book. In Chapter 2,
on September the 3rd, 1939, with the 'King's Speech' and the
world on the brink of war, the Victorian superstructure was
decadent. Winston Churchill rescued the superstructure
somewhat by becoming the political leader of Britain, "Onwards,
Christian Soldiers" was his favourite hymn by all accounts, and
the 'secret societies' could find new activities amidst the murky
darkness of the miasma, but the ideology and consciousness of
the British Empire was definitely waning. The Second World War
was a victory for global capitalism under the superstructure of
the USA and not the British. One could argue that a social
revolution happened in Britain after World War II with the
Labour government and the social reform programmes, even
though some may still deny their importance (e.g. economic
rationalists). In contrast, and in 1877, with the declaration of
empire by Disraeli and the continued ruling stability of the reign
of Queen Victoria, the Victorian superstructure was at its height,
and the notion of Englishness seemed to rule the world, because
being English and from the upper classes was a passport to
wealth and power. 'Being English' included a notion of fair play,
the concept of being a 'gentleman', sacrifice for the good of the
nation and interacting positively and loyally with the other
members of your class from the 'secret societies' of your school,
and in the more general 'old boy's clubs' in society. Social
revolution did not happen in 1877 because the inter-relationships
between separate elements of the superstructure such as the

singing of the hymn, "Onwards, Christian Soldiers" and the 'secret societies' were strongly immanent and unquestioned. When a BBC commentator on the side of the Thames declared that the atmosphere in London was "positively Victorian", as he was describing the Royal Flotilla of 2012, the recreation of the Victorian superstructure was the point that he wanted to make. He sensed something historical, powerful, extended, expansionist and patriotic about the flag waving and water borne procession. His words give testament to the fact that in his mind that historical ersatz cultural event of 2012 was more evocative than real life, wherein the Victorian superstructure had dissipated. In the next chapter, we will look at the ways in which the Victorian superstructure was emergent and under construction during the industrial revolution of 1815-1825 and social revolution nearly happened.

Social revolution did not happen in 1877 Britain, because the Victorian superstructure stopped the downtrodden and exploited from rising up and challenging the ruling powerful elite. Of course, it takes more than ideology or consciousness to achieve this, the Victorian superstructure was backed up by a new police force, the numerous brigades of the British land army, the vast navy reserves and the innumerable laws that were directed against the lower and working classes, e.g. the debtors' laws. What is interesting from an immanent materialist perspective is how the outward movement and prospects of the British Empire in 1877 are directly complemented by the ways in which the system worked in terms of domestication, repression and suppression. There is a morality and code of ethics that comes with the notions of 'being English' and taking part in the expansion of the British Empire that revels in 'fair play', heroism and feats of physical, emotional and intellectual prowess. This code plays out in reverse as a means to exacerbate the ways in which the downtrodden and repressed are not able to live up to such highly mannered expectations. The most obvious way that this mechanism works is to trap individuals and groups from the lower and working classes in their own talents and wills to power through criminality, prison and the meshing of gang mentalities. To break free of the shackles of servitude that involved being in a difficult and lowly economic position from birth, the members of the Victorian under-classes had to break laws. Such action was characterised not only by breaking laws that involved murder, theft or fraud, but also through a whole plethora of civil and social laws that had been evolved through the establishment of Victorian 'polite' society, and that came to be known as the 'manners' of the English. These manners were rigorously taught and reinforced by the elites through the public schools and a raft of social, sporting and civil events that were established in the Victorian period. The truth was that it didn't matter how talented or skilled you were, if one had not been trained how to behave and speak at such events, one was excluded and ridiculed.

One can therefore understand that Marx was right and wrong with respect to the social production of identity and the Victorian superstructure. He was right with respect to the ways in which social production was tied to economic progress and change. In 1877 and with the declaration of empire, one can understand how an entire global capitalist enterprise was functioning well and this favoured the British who controlled international finance, shipping routes, factory production and consumption through the introduction of branding. Yet this whole gigantic enterprise only favoured those who partook and shared in the aforementioned 'Englishness' and who understood its specific codes. For example, Disraeli, the favourite of Queen Victoria, became thoroughly English as Prime Minister and the Earl of Beaconsfield, and he lived out the life of an English gentleman on his estate and in Parliament, despite his often cruel depiction in the British media as being the Jewish 'Shylock'. Disraeli existed in his later life within the Victorian superstructure, and one could indeed surmise that he was one of its principal architects. Yet

Marx was wrong to think that this 1877 historical correlation between the social production of identity and economics was absolute. Disraeli may well have been a brilliant actor, who picked up on the mannerisms and artifice of the English without truly believing in them. At heart, he may well have always been an outsider to the Victorian superstructure, as was Marx, even though both Disraeli and Marx both understood how the super-structure worked better than most. What we should focus on is not only the generalised economic modes of production of identity that were at play in 1877, but the specific ways in which the pretence and dream of 'being English' were enacted. Such modes of identity-becoming are performed beyond and through the highly rational ways in which Marx and Disraeli were merged with the Victorian superstructure by living out their lives, Disraeli as politician, writer and protector of the empire, Marx as a social activist, analyst and critic. The specific modes of English pretence and dreams bring into the frame of this chapter on the Queen Victoria/Disraeli 1877 plane of immanence, darker, but no less essential aspects of the English character that concern the occult.

English occultism

The official religion of the British Empire in 1877 was Anglican Christianity as represented and personified by the hymn, "Onward, Christian Soldiers" above. Such a hymn leads to a drab association with militarism and a herd mentality that fears the other and incorporates explicit and covert forms of racism into its *modus operandi*. Clearly, this type of religion is not powerful or spiritually exciting enough for the sons of the 'secret societies' as described by Cecil Rhodes above. The private religion of the British Empire heroes was far more complex and interesting than mainstream Christianity because it was a secret; in contrast, Christianity was meant for the conformism of empire workers. The philosophical work of Thomas Hill Green and his successors who functioned in the British idealist mode, mainly gave rise to university debate in terms of Christian metaphysics and the physics of the idea according to Plato. Such idealism may have been interesting to the 'secret societies' of the British Empire, but the dry intellectualism of the debate would have escaped their full attention, as did the recourses to moral self-actualisation that were represented by Victorian civil society and philanthropy. The 'secret societies' were composed of men primarily interested in power, travel and exoticism, money, sex and increasing their social/cultural influence. The occult was seen as a means to gain these results and was practised in various manners in the vaults of stately homes, clubs and in the private chapels of the British Empire. To understand how the specifics of English occultism relates to the immanence of the plane of Queen Victoria/Disraeli 1877, and to the immanent materialism of this book, it is useful to look at the life of perhaps the most famous English occultist, Aleister Crowley.

Crowley was born in Leamington Spa in 1875. He was a product of the Victorian superstructure and the particular energetics of the age that we are currently examining in terms of immanence and their relevance to the 'capitalised education' of Kate Middleton. Crowley rebelled against the Christianity of his parents, and set off on his strange journey into the occult as a young man at the University of Cambridge. Crowley changed his name, experimented with drugs and promiscuity, wrote poetry, took up mountaineering, studied literature, philosophy and religion, and eventually joined the Order of the Golden Dawn. Crowley has become famous as an occultist, who wrote about and practised 'Magick' as he termed it and his infamy has led to comments such as this one that was fortunately omitted by Melville as direct speech for Captain Ahab: "In one sense, Aleister Crowley is lower than whale shit. In another, he's as high as God's hat. The true shaman knows that God's hat is made out of dried whale shit,"[43]. Crowley is a truly contradictory character and one suitable to understand the products of the Victorian superstructure, whose base we need to be able to depict from an immanent materialist perspective. For example, Crowley revelled in being called 'the Beast' by his mother, yet took individuals to court for defamation if they dared to accuse him of Satanism. The truth of the matter was that English occultism of the kind practised by Crowley was possible due to the material wealth generated by the functioning of the British Empire. The height of the British Empire, which is perhaps represented by the 1877, Queen Victoria/Disraeli plane of immanence, also includes a strain of cosmopolitan decadence that allows for and creates the kind of occultism that was practised by Aleister Crowley and his peers.

This 'cosmopolitan decadence' of English occultism adds to our understanding of the immanence of the plane of 1877, and also shows why the superstructure of the British Empire was superseded by American capitalist ideology by 1939. Put simply, the push to build and maintain the British Empire, the ability to own the extensive and spread out British territories of the time— and to control the international world economy through financial, diplomatic and military means—was too much to handle for the English psyche all at once. The realisation of the will to power in the terms of the material facts of the British Empire and the opportunities that this expansion brought the British elite, encouraged feelings of being 'God-like' and unassailability to a mode of consciousness that was paradoxically steeped in amateurism and 'fair play'. At the heart of the British Empire there was an instability and strangeness that could lead to an otherness in oneself. Crowley's exotic occultism, which was an attempt to revive and live out forgotten religious rites, such as those found in the cultures of ancient Egypt, Greece, India and Israel, presents an impossibly alien series of practises, beliefs and ideals to itself. Yet it is this alienation and strangeness that is precisely the point in terms of the immanent materialism that this chapter must analyse and depict from the perspective of Queen Victoria/Disraeli in 1877. The British Empire needed an underbelly of weirdness in order to cohere in terms of the breadth and depth of its operations. The stifling boredom of English civil society, with its complex social rules and regulations, manners and 'stiff upper lip' attitude to most things, was girded and permeated by the excess and expenditure of the occult. The point is not as if Crowley and his peers invented a wholly new means to live, but the will that was impelling British subjects to exploit the fruits of the British Empire also gave rise to the occult possibilities as exemplified by, for example, Crowley.

Indeed, Crowley specifically mentions that his occult system of 'Magick' was a practise that was intended to enhance will power[44]. One can understand this assertion with respect to, for example, the Hindu tradition of yoga and how, if done correctly, it would enhance and sustain concentration and resolve. It is when Crowley deploys the more fanciful aspects of ancient Egyptian religion, Qabbalism, and his mystical laws that one begins to query, doubt and comprehend the over extension of English occultism. As an antidote to the dull repetition of "Onward, Christian Soldiers", the practise of Crowley's 'Magick' comes as a welcome change and as a revitalising religious code that should not lead to a closed minded attitude to life. Yet as a coherent practise and organised system for understanding the secrets of life, English occultism of the type put forward by Crowley often fails to deliver the perceived benefits of enhanced will power, insight and revelation. This is because Crowley himself perceived his new Thelemaic religion as a transcendental and obscurist replacement to Christianity, rather than aligning its practise to actual increases in power that were immanent to the plane of 1877 and through the British Empire. One could say that Crowley's occultism represents a form of wastage and decadence that was written into the plane of 1877 by the often amateurish and somewhat odd practises of the British ruling elite. One can contrast this system with, for example, the ways in which the German Nazi Party under the leadership of Adolf Hitler and Joseph Goebbels used the occult to accompany and enhance their economically driven yet racially motivated National Socialism of the 1930s (see chapter 5). The immanence of English occultism wasn't tied to economic drives, but separate from them due to the British class structure, educational training in the classics (idealism), and the global success of the British Empire in 1877 and beyond, that effectively cleared the British upper classes of any financial woes. The fear of destitution was concentrated in every social class of 1877 other than the top echelons, and Marx perceived this enormous fear in the masses as the means to revolutionary action. Yet this fear had another side that was being acted out immanently through the principles of social Darwinism.

Social Darwinism

Unlike the English occultism of Crowley and others, the system of Darwin's evolutionary theory was founded on scientifically provable principles. Darwin was sixty-eight years old in 1877 — his *On the Origins of the Species* had been published in 1859, and had received widespread interest and notoriety by the 1870s along with other publications of Darwin's such as *The Descent of Man*. Now, as we look back at Charles Darwin, we see him as the father of modern evolutionary theory that has had enormous influence and impact in the study of sciences such as biology, anthropology and palaeontology. Yet in 1877, the impact of Darwin's ideas was perhaps most keenly felt in the social field, wherein the debates about human origin, race, social selection and breeding had been raging. The thesis under public discussion in 1877 was whether or not the white British upper classes had got to their lofty and privileged positions by the definition of natural selection as described by Darwin or through some 'godly' powers. This discussion was accompanied by the assumptions of racism, or at least that the white Christian colonialists and their civilisation was superior to others; and misogyny, in that men had evolved to a superior form to women through natural selection. Darwin himself did not ascribe to these views, yet they were instrumental in terms of many of the social organisations that ruled society. For example, women could not vote in 1877 or take part in politics, and this continued inequality was justified by some on Darwinian grounds. The fear embedded in the argument of social Darwinism was directed against what is naturally occurring and not man-made, and what was perceived to be lowly, malformed, 'animal-like', inarticulate or poor.

One might look back in horror at social Darwinism, especially as it was associated with and adapted by the Nazi Party in Germany in the 1930s, where social Darwinism was deployed to justify their purification of the human species on Germanic grounds (see chapter 5). However, one should not doubt the continued and extended impact of social Darwinism in terms of the immanence of the plane of 1877. The 'within-ness' of the plane locates a fear of the 'animal other' that became widespread and communicable through the internationalisation of the British Empire. One might say that social Darwinism had become a folk myth through this fear, no longer readily accountable to the scientific and empirical data that was used by Darwin to construct his theory of evolution and the principles of natural selection, yet possible to incorporate into judgements about character, self-worth, education, race and class. The transfer-ability and adaptability of social Darwinism has become lodged in the ideologies and work practises of, for example, British professionals working abroad, who have been deployed and accepted around the world since 1877, and are a testament of the perception of natural selection in professional life as a guiding principle of scientific method and ability. For example, university qualifications from Oxford and Cambridge are still a passport to employment and opportunities beyond their domestic English locations. The intellectual hierarchy that this statement implies is based upon assumptions of quality, rigour and scientific truth, and not predicated on the underlying apparatuses of elitism, exclusion and class consciousness that still exist in the United Kingdom today. The point of contention here is a complex one, which can be elaborated and explained through understanding how the plateau of Queen Victoria/Disraeli 1877 inter-relates to a climate of fear that was spread via the British Empire and in the guise of social Darwinism.

Famous cartoons at the time depict Darwin as an ape man and give us some insight into the immanent effects of the climate of fear in the British Empire of 1877[45]. The fear of the other is a fear of 'animalism', of instinct taking over and dominating the motives of man, of the rough, of the possibly unhygienic, of the sexual and of the irrational. Even though Charles Darwin was perhaps one of the most assiduously careful of scientific investigators, whose insights into the processes of evolution have largely been proved to be right, the association of his ideas in society with animal debasement was prevalent. This is because the implications of evolutionary theory contravened the basic assumptions that mankind was somehow God-given, unique (i.e. not an animal), and in possession of a spiritual self or soul, in short, all attitudes and ideas that are derived from idealism. The challenge of Darwinian materialism to the widespread belief in the god-like image of man caused a rupture in societal thinking that still has implications and echoes today in arguments and discussions about man's place on the Earth. For example, some might argue that the monarch's place in society is immutable and God-given, others might argue for social Darwinism as described above, which justifies the ways in which the monarch has been able to get to the top of society and maintain his or her position through natural selection, i.e. the monarchy is somehow 'natural'. The truth of the matter is that Darwinian materialism shows us the random ways in which some species survive and others do not. There is nothing God-given or special about the monarchy or mankind in general, other than what is bestowed on individuals or groups by the rest of society. In corollary, we make the monarchy 'God-like' through our aspirations...

In contrast, Darwin was depicted as an ape, even though he was perhaps one of the greatest scientists that has ever lived. This shows the pervasiveness of the fear of the 'animal-other' that Darwin had provoked with his new theory of evolution, and how the climate of fear against the animal-other was defended and upheld by prevailing Victorian social milieu. The immanence of the plane of Queen Victoria/Disraeli 1877 spread this fear out and made it a commonplace belief around the world. This is because the British Empire and the capitalist system that worked at its economic heart created networks, alliances, allegiances and systems which acted as two way modes of communication and formed inter-relationships. Of course, one could view the image of Darwin as an ape and react against it as being merely satirical, or dismiss such a caricature in favour of a rigorous assessment of Darwin's life and work. However, the point of analysis in terms of immanence works against the ways in which one is able to stand back and refute such imagery as being harmless. In fact, such imagery is far from harmless, as it carries it with it profound social messages that were aimed against animality, savagery and nativism and that were enacted through the creation of 'human zoos'. Immanence sweeps through such drawings as Darwin as an ape, because humour sometimes unleashes unconscious and collective thoughts that determine aspects of social life and behaviour. In this instance, what we see are the ways in which animal nature had been connected to a scientist who uncovered the continuum from animals to humans. The immanence of the picture also works on the social level, wherein the 'life of the poor', i.e. animals, has been represented as the body, whereas the privileged, i.e. the rich, white, colonial, male scientist is the head. The life of the poor and the widespread climate of fear that this life engendered, helps to form the immanence of the plane of Queen Victoria/Disraeli in 1877.

The life of the poor

Charles Darwin and Aleister Crowley were very different characters who had two things in common. They were both English and they both had access to capital. Without the access to capital, they would not have been able to develop their antipathetic yet oddly complementary intellectual endeavours. If Charles Darwin and Aleister Crowley had been born into 'the life of the poor', we would not have a Darwinian theory of evolution or any remnants of Crowley's Thelemaic religion today. Instead, they would have lived their days out as anonymous male workers, focussing all their intellectual, emotional and physical strength on the continual battle to feed themselves and their families through the minimal wages that their work would have brought in. The life of the poor was not an educated life, but was set against the harsh and unjust economic reality of the time, wherein the global success of the British Empire acted as a feedback mechanism that primarily fed into the power, maintenance and development of the upper classes in society. There was some governmental movement in terms of 'educating the masses' at the time, but this push for educational reform did not seriously take off until after World War II. The life of the poor, and the state of antagonism which existed between the rich and the poor in 1877 was summarised by Disraeli in 1845 in his political novel:

> Two nations between whom there is no intercourse and no sympathy; who are ignorant of each other's habits, thoughts and feelings, as if they were dwellers in different zones or inhabitants of different planets; who are formed by different breeding, are fed by different food, are ordered by different manners, and are not governed by the same laws[46].

If anything, the situation had become worse by 1877 in terms of the disparities in wealth, privilege and power between the two nations as described by Disraeli in 1845. Such stark dualism between the rich and the poor was underpinned by the climate of fear that was prevalent in 1877 and is still relevant to the 'capitalised education' of Kate Middleton today. The fear of poverty, being labelled as poor, or even coming from 'poor stock' as the ideology of social Darwinism might put it, has latterly propelled English families such as Middleton's upwards in their quest for economic security, mobility and social acceptability (see chapter 7). Such 'category jumping' between the 'life of the poor' and the 'life of the rich' was much more difficult in 1877 than it is now, even though it is hardly easy today, and as the excerpt from *Sybil* suggests, was compounded by the ways in which the divisions between rich and poor were considered and maintained as absolute. Kate's family have been able to reinvent themselves, as they have gained access to capital through inheritance and the success of their online party planning business, as they have paid for high quality private education for their children, and as they have been inculcated into the upper echelons of societal life in Britain. In contrast, the life of the poor in 1877 was characterised by populations having very little education, associations with gangs and crime, precarious living conditions, hunger, violence and alcohol fuelled drunkenness. This was a life where the climate of fear prevailed, and in a parallel manner to the miasma described in the previous chapter, gave rise to misunder-standings, short-sightedness, a lack of sound judgement and an effervescent bubbling of emotion and reactivity. Living the life of the poor meant at the same time being susceptible to the ways in which the rich maintained and increased their positions of power.

Marx described this process through the analysis of labour relations. The control of labour relations by the rich to create surplus value and profit from their British Empire enterprises in 1877 made the fact of low wages more than a statistical or historical anomaly. Being involved with 'the life of the poor' had definite consequences in terms of identity, self-esteem, community engagement, linguistic and literate abilities, health, aspiration and hope. Marx reconciled these interconnected consequences of the life of the poor through the notion of alienation; and alienation came about primarily because workers on the wrong side of labour relations as controlled by the capitalist owners of industry and property, had no say in what labouring meant[47]. In consequence, the capitalised rich could make the poor work as hard as they wanted, pay the workers a minimum subsistence wage, and restrict their living conditions through tenancy. Marx saw the negative consequences of industrialisation and capital on the life of the poor through the lens of alienation, because the poor became automata, working their whole lives without insight into the truths of capitalism or the possibility of self-realisation into the harm that was being done to them. Marx saw first-hand what this alienation meant, as he lived in London in 1877, yet he did have access to capital through his wife's family, and we only have his analysis of capitalism today because he could survive due to his wife's inheritance. Marx was not himself a laboured worker, but provides a convincing analysis of what life was like for the poor at the time through his depictions of factory-life, labour relations and alienation. This analysis provides the basis for understanding the material immanence of the life of the poor on the Queen Victoria/Disraeli plane of 1877. Another valuable insight into the life of the poor in 1877 comes from the Irish playwright and intellectual who had recently moved to London, George Bernard Shaw.

Shaw was a committed socialist and joined the Fabian Society in 1884. Shaw was a prodigious writer of essays, novels, pamphlets, plays and letters. However, in opposition to the prevailing Victorian fashion of the time, he did not see the purpose of his output as becoming popular, to make money or to merely entertain. Rather, Shaw wholeheartedly engaged with the discussions and debates that concerned the social problems of the time, many of which have run through this chapter on the immanence of the Queen Victoria/Disraeli plane in 1877. With respect to the poor, and according to Shaw, because men were fully occupied by their professions and in a constant battle for survival, however badly paid, the key to revolutionising the life of the poor lay with the women. In Shaw's most famous and popular play, *Pygmalion*, the female protagonist, Eliza Doolittle, becomes the object of a wager by a professor of phonetics, Henry Higgins. Higgins bets that he could enable Eliza to pass as a duchess at an ambassador's garden party by focussing solely on her spoken language, and transforming Eliza's cockney speech into standard received English. However, one's memories and thoughts about the play are perhaps impinged upon by the 1960s film version called *My Fair Lady*, which was itself based on a 1950s Broadway musical version. The various adaptations of the play have lessened the political and emancipatory aspects of the work that Shaw had intended to prevail, and have focussed instead on the romantic, comedic elements of the situation. Eliza is progressively transformed into an object of desire by the various post-Shaw *Pygmalion* treatments, she is no longer the revolutionary and feminist figure that Shaw had initially conceptualised and created, and, perhaps even more tellingly, the relationships between Eliza and Higgins and his assistant are transformed in the later versions into a quasi-romantic love triangle.

Shaw's point of writing the play *Pygmalion* is to show that social change is possible through the emancipation of women[48]. In other words, the life of the poor can be bettered through the education of women and the ways in which this education will change the modes in which women see and act in the world. Importantly for Shaw, emancipated women would choose better spouses, and this improved choice would progressively lead to the betterment of the working classes through selective breeding. This is in contrast to Marx's view of violent revolution as being the only way to change the lot of the poor under capitalism[49]. In short, we are left with a conundrum with respect to the life of the poor and the immanence relevant to the plane of Queen Victoria/Disraeli 1877. Marx was right in that violent proletariat revolution has led to the poor having increased possibilities for life in Russia, China and Cuba. Shaw was also right in that the post-war educational revolution in the UK of women and others has led to increased working class possibilities and escape routes from the servitude and drudgery of the 1877 life of the poor. The problem with Marx's communist solution, is that it has proved to be unsustainable in the context of global capitalism and the world market, the problem with Shaw's 'education of the masses' is that the envelopment of world capitalism has meant that many highly educated and skilled professionals have found themselves overqualified and underemployed in the current state of world affairs dominated by finance. The immanence of the plane of Queen Victoria/Disraeli in 1877 that corresponds to the life of the poor, sits somewhere in between the revolution of Marx, which required strong leadership, an understanding of ideology and combinational social organisation against the ruling capitalist power base, and the education of Shaw, which necessitated a concerted effort to understand and implement the learning needs of the disenfranchised. In summary, one could characterise this aspect of the immanence of the plane of 1877 in terms of a 'becoming-revolutionary' that is directed towards Victorianism.

Conclusion

This chapter and plateau sits as a high-point in the construction of British identity, and the identity underpinnings of KM as media object and a capitalised education that this book is heading towards. However, as we have seen, this high-point is not without its low-points and there is a terrific gap between the high and the low. Such a differentiated situation that we find in 1877 can only lead to collapse, and indeed, the power of the British Empire is effectively under erasure by the time of the plateau in chapter 2 of September the 3rd, 1939. However in 1877, the precise factors and historical situation that were reached in 1939 was inconceivable, as Britain had spent several centuries fighting off the competition of the rival European nations such as France, Spain and the Netherlands, and ruled the world through diplomacy, capitalism, the army and naval power. This plateau, as the zenith in British power in this book, connects most closely with the next, chapter 4, where the problems, benefits and changes to British society that were produced by technological development and the economic use of this technology are closely analysed. Chapter 4 lays the conditions for chapter 3 to be possible, and ultimately for the power of KM as media object and a capitalised education to be fully achieved. This is because KM as media object is part of the machine and learning processes that currently work on and contort subjectivity under capitalism.

Chapter 4

Taken apart at the seams —'teachers':

The industrial revolution—1815-1825

Introduction

The plateau of 1877 presents a zenith in terms of the ways in which the British Empire was able to project and maintain power. The period in Britain from 1815-1825 provides a crucial build up and platform to 1877 in terms of the intensification in industrialisation and the effects of industrialisation on social life in the UK. With respect to the immanent materialism of this book, the manner in which the industrial revolution dislocated and separated the subject and tied it to machines is recurrent and relevant with respect to the latest digital machines and contemporary forms of socialisation. One might say that we learn about the machine processes that partially explain how we are subjectified and turned into consumers in the globally inter-related marketplace via events such as the royal wedding of April the 29th, 2011, by studying the period of 1815-1825. In other words, the media object, Kate Middleton or (KM) and a capitalised education can relate to, enter into and indirectly influence our psyches, because we have already been opened up to this possibility by the forms in which machines have become integral to our mental functioning on the cognitive, affective or mechanical levels. The plateau of 1815-1825 is critical to these processes, because new and powerful forms of technological innovation were being harnessed and progressed through coal-powered steam machinery, and this activity was unprecedented and accelerated. The bustling construction of factories, urban housing, municipal buildings, new and faster modes of transport on water and on land and the means to distribute these forms of transport such as bridges, roads and canals, were cutting a combined swathe through what it meant to exist and what socialisation amounted to. In particular, the discovery that huge profits could be made from and due to industrial technology, motivated and uprooted entire populations, and this uprooting still carries on today as the urbanisation of the human race continues without relent. This chapter explores these forces and factors in social and economic life, as it constructs the plateau of 1815-1825, and examines the ways in which the immanent materialism of these processes connects to facets of our lives now. In line with the immanent materialism of this book, the perspective that this chapter paints is not wholly negative, even though the social and cultural effects of factory and mechanised life will not be overlooked or ignored because these effects can be truly repetitive and deadening, uncreative and leading to a dreadful sense of boredom. This point of abjection is why the plateau of 1815-1825, that spans 10 years of industrial and social history, includes the figure of the teacher, to complement the facts of subjective rearrangement that accompanied the accelerated combinations of coal and steam powered machines within the push to commercial and industrial success.

The teacher today has to negotiate a plethora of social, cultural and governmental interests that can 'tear them apart' as they go about their everyday jobs[50]. For example, the task of classroom management in urban areas can be life threatening, understanding the exact learning needs of globalised heterogeneous populations can lead to madness. In short, the notion of a sealed, unified mode of consciousness necessary to negotiate the current demands of the teaching profession is impossible. A particularly revealing strategy to understand such dismemberment and tearing apart is to try to think through how machines and social life have collided and become progressively more complexly intertwined since the field of interaction was relatively emergent in the period between 1815-1825 in Britain.

The teacher sits inside an apparatus of complex machinery every time he or she enters into the immanent field of teaching and learning. This chapter is therefore an attempt to disentangle aspects of the extraordinary human-machine entanglements that have been passed down by generations living, working, thinking and existing in relation to and through machines. The point of the plateau of 1815-1825 and the immanent materialist analysis contained here is not to return to a pure or unified teacher, or to reconstruct a teaching and learning vestibule or sanctuary lurking behind the intervention through history by machinery, but to examine the holes, gaps, speeds and mutational forms of mechanical reference that are contained in the plateau. Once that work has been done, the emergent field of 1815-1825 will be made immanent in terms of discovering a 'withinness' of machinery that has valency today.

The pressure within – 'steam-power'

The technology of steam-powered engines was ready for proliferation in Britain by 1815. James Watt's eighteenth-century work on making the steam engine more efficient proved to be one of the great innovations that powered the industrial revolution of the nineteenth century. The machinic processes at the heart of the steam-engine are the heating up of water by burning coal, which drives pistons that turns wheels capable of doing the mechanical work previously done by human labour, horses and environmental energy sources such as wind and water. Watt's engines were smaller, more efficient and could be located away from natural sources of water, making the building and positioning of factories more flexible and able to spread out across the nation. The consolidation of the stream-engine by Watt contributed to Sadi Carnot's approach to a hypothetical heat engine (1824)[51], which theorised the isothermic properties of the heat engine. Carnot's theorem is a formal statement of this fact: *No engine operating between two heat reservoirs can be more efficient than a*

Carnot engine operating between the same reservoirs. This maximum efficiency $\eta = 1$ is defined to be:

Where:
$$\eta = \frac{W}{Q_H} = 1 - \frac{T_C}{T_H} \tag{1}$$

W is the work done by the system (energy exiting the system as work),

Q_H is the heat put into the system (heat energy entering the system),

T_C is the absolute temperature of the cold reservoir, and

T_H is the absolute temperature of the hot reservoir.

A corollary to Carnot's theorem states that: *All reversible engines operating between the same heat reservoirs are equally efficient.* Carnot's theorem eventually became incorporated into the second law of thermodynamics, which defines the entropy of a system, or the point of thermodynamic equilibrium or heat exchange of the system. According to the second law of thermo-dynamics, the entropy of a natural system is irreversible, yet reversibility is a convenient theoretical fiction or ideal state. Entropy can also be defined as the disorder in the universe or the availability of the energy in the system to do work, and it is a measure of a system's thermal energy per unit temperature that is unavailable for doing useful work. The development of the dynamics of the steam-engine, from the actual technological innovations made by Watt in terms of efficiency, to the mathe-matical consolidation of Carnot and the formulation of the second law of thermodynamics and entropy, have important consequences in terms of the immanent materialism of this chapter that concerns the plateau of 1815-1825. These conse-quences came about because the base workings of the heat-exchange-steam-machines caused a pressurized revolution in social-cultural/working life that is still unfurling and happening today.

James Watt came up with a modified and effective coal-driven steam engine in 1754, and this invention progressively replaced muscle and environmental power in factories[52]. There followed a mass migration of workers from rural farms to the 'dark Satanic Mills' of industrialized cities in Britain, and this movement was accompanied by appalling working and living conditions, which generated a host of deficiency diseases and infections. These were first reported by Friedrich Engels in his classic publication, *The Condition of the Working Class in England* (1845). To facilitate the transport of goods and people, in 1829 George Stephenson invented the first workable steam locomotive, named The Rocket. This engine and its carriages ran on the Liverpool-Manchester railway, it was opened by the Prime Minister of the day, the Duke of Wellington, and tragically killed a local MP on its first trip. Steam-power was launched on the railway lines and through the transport networks in Britain and latterly throughout the world. These irreversible processes are impinging upon the environment today, as the effects of steam pressured heat engine have been transformed through successive waves of mechanical revolution that started in the period of 1815-1825 in Britain with the steam-engine and the steam locomotive.

The implications of steam-power of the plateau of 1815-1825 have been vast and wide ranging. One can point to the urbanisation of the human race, the evacuation and devastation of rural communities, global warming, the depletion of fossil fuels, which began with the exploitation of coal to fire the heat engines of the industrial revolution, and has led to the global economic dependence on coal, oil, petrol and the heat exchanges of contemporary energy creation and usage. One could state that the mathematical equation of the Carnot engine has created the understanding and conditions that still drive much of the industrial production and consumption today, from factory production in 'developing' countries such as China and India, to the transportation of goods by air, road and sea. The Carnot equation and second law of thermodynamics still govern much of the machinic activity on the planet, including the continued working and design of coal-fired power stations and the running of multitudinous vehicles such as cars, trucks and aeroplanes that are conspiring to warm up the planet further through the environmental release of carbon dioxide. Carnot, Watt and Stephenson could not possibly have conceived of the consequences of their innovative technological and mathematical work, yet in terms of immanent materialism there is a direct relationship between the development in steam-power in 1815-1825 in Britain due to the industrial revolution and contemporary environmental, economic and social crises. It is as if we have the abstract machinery of the Carnot equation in our collective imaginations as a guide and rule to the thermodynamic heat exchanges that are dominating the latest phase of global history, which has been described recently as the anthropocene[53]. The 'pressure within' due to the emergence of industrialisation from the steam-engine and onwards has developed to such an extent and with such speed that all global activity is now connected in some way to Carnot and entropy: for example, the sale of Amazonian rainforest to Chinese oil companies, or the expansion of coal ports on the Queensland coast close to the Great Barrier Reef. The abstract machinery of the second law of thermodynamics provides an understanding of successive tipping points, wherein the processes of increasing and combinational industrialisation have caused crises, acceleration and disruption in world events. All of the smaller, individual engines of industrial progress under globally connected capitalism are contributing to the present one world system of international heat exchange. Yet at the same time that the work efficiency of the steam-engine of Watt, the mathematical heat exchange of Carnot and the propulsion engine of Stephenson came together through abstraction and a form of industrial capitalism, rebellion and resistance to these forces of globalisation was made possible. One might describe the emergent and therefore immanent qualities of this resistance in two ways:

1) The agrarian response to steam-power

The enormous movement of people from rural and agricultural regions to the new industrial cityscapes that were dominated by factories did not happen without resistance. The 'dark Satanic Mills' as described by William Blake in the preface to his *Milton, a Poem,* was possibly a reference to the Albion Flour Mill in London, which was powered by one of the first Watt and Boulton (Watt's commercial partner) rotary steam-engines. The structure and form of the agrarian lifestyle, which had been constituted for hundreds of years within the confines and under the rubric of the feudal system in Europe, was put under enormous pressure due to the explosion of inter-connected industrial and commercial activity between 1815-1825. Certainly, on the negative side of the agrarian equation, there was widespread poverty, a lack of education, malnutrition and related health issues and a sense of isolation in the rural landscape, yet the agrarian life simultaneously constituted a connection with nature, community and an appreciation of what is vigorous in the 'outdoors' life. In contrast, the life of work in the new factories run by steam-power was physically hard, repetitive, unhealthy and led to the potentially negative internalisation of thought and a disconnection with the natural biosphere. Workers in factories were exploited by the rise of a class of new industrial owners, who ran their factories to make a profit, and paid the workers the minimum possible wage in order to benefit themselves, the sale price of their products, and their resultant place in the emergent capitalist markets where the goods were sold. One straightforward agrarian response to the rise of steam-power and the new factories governed by market forces during the industrial revolution was simply that the situation was unjust.

Perhaps the most enduring and famous agrarian response to steam-power came through the short-lived Luddite movement, which sought to physically destroy the new machines and the interconnected thermodynamic processes. However, it has been convincingly argued that the Luddites were not in fact anti-machine, but anti-starvation and anti-unemployment, as their uprising coincides with the harsh economic conditions imposed upon Britain by the cost of fighting the Napoleonic Wars[54]. In fact, the Luddites smashed machines as a protest against these working conditions and not against the inventions of Watt and Stephenson *per se*. One should understand the rise of the Luddites as a continuum and in an historical context, wherein protest and upheaval was commonplace, and various social movements had been fighting continuously against unjust working conditions, and not just the interpolation of steam-powered machines on their lives. One could, in this vein, argue that the Luddites were preceded by the organised industrial action of the stockingers since 1675 and were succeeded by the general Chartist movement in the nineteenth century and beyond. The interpolation of the steam-engine machine on lifestyle and thought is therefore submerged beneath an ongoing continuum of reactivity against industrial hardship and unfairness, rather than having any transversal, crossover effects, such as those described in chapter 1 in the section on 'cyborg capitalism'. The point, however, of this immanent materialist analysis, is not to seek determinate origins in behaviour, or to assign causal effects, such as the Luddites smashed machines because of x, y and z. The point here is to construct an immanent material analysis of the plane of 1815-1825. In and through that plane, the Luddites and their successors were players in the agrarian response to steam-power and the infiltration of Watt, Stephenson and Carnot in the workings of everyday life the power of factories. In many ways, the Luddites were part of the thermodynamic equation introduced by steam-power, their violent action was driven by the 'pressure within' produced by the efficiency gains of Watt, the equations of Carnot and the second law of thermodynamics. In other words, their aggressive action was part of the general uptake in society of mechanisation.

This last point about mechanisation could be extrapolated to today, and the response against mechanisation includes all the revolutions, upheavals and violent demonstrations that have irrupted around working conditions that have manifested in the world during and since 1815-1825. The unprecedented evolution and interconnection in machinery and economic development that has happened since Watt and Stephenson, and that has morphed into the anthropocene, has enabled a consistent field of operations through which social grievance may be expressed. For example, the toxic industrial landscape and sweat-shop mentality that is present in some parts of China, and particularly where there is a concentration of factories, is bound to result in unionisation and protest at the continued working conditions, low pay and stifling, disciplinary culture. The steam-engines of Watt and Boulton have long since been replaced, but the basic mode of factory organisation and lifestyle is still present, and defines a form of becoming that one may connect to the industrial revolution of 1815-1825 in Britain. The analytic and synthetic modes of immanent materialism allow for and encourage these connections and add layers and depth to the mode of representation and resultant politics on offer. Perhaps one could say with conviction that few in the UK today want to devote their lives to the repetitive drudge of factory existence which was brought into existence during the period of 1815-1825. The reality of office life has equally lost its shine since the 1980s liberal revolution in PCs has led to countless screen dominated office jobs being created in businesses around the world. What we are left with at the end of analysis and as a practical, physical reaction to steam-power, Carnot, thermodynamics and entropy is the agrarian response as an escape, a longing for a simpler life, away from the build-up of machinery and the continued pressure of the mechanosphere on the frailty of thought, imagination and desire.

2) The intellectual challenge to steam-power

At the start of the nineteenth century, perhaps the most enduring intellectual movement in Britain and Europe to challenge steam-power, and one that has contemporary relevance, was romanticism. To be part of this movement, one had to be able to avoid the servitude of factory or rural life, and without widespread educational provision, intellectual life was only accessible with inherited or gained wealth. Romanticism could be defined by the intellectual and artistic responses to the mechanisation of life, represented here on the plateau of 1815-1825 through steam-power and the 'pressure within'. The agrarian response to social mechanisation could be presented as a form of collective brute energy, whereas the romantic response took this brute energy and made something aesthetic, creative and intellectual out of it, whether it were in words, mathematics, painting or music. The perspicuous romantic position was that there is always something missing from a mechanised rendering of the universe, and this 'something' is accessible via the genius of poetry, philosophy, music and art. One could frame the exact nature of the romantic missing element in the world as an explanatory challenge to science, which had accelerated and intensified in the early part of the nineteenth century through the wide recognition of the mathematical work of the Enlightenment. One could argue that the developments in steam-power, Carnot's heat-engine and understanding of the second law of thermodynamics and entropy, which in turn led to the construction of factories in the industrial revolution, were paralleled by advances in science, measurement and calculation. Romanticism challenged the domination of these external disciplines in that constructive or destructive creativity, and the understanding of the self was not a formative or fundamental aspect of the industrial programmes. Furthermore, romanticism arose in opposition to the stability thesis of the Newtonian universe, wherein stable laws directed the ways in which bodies related and worked with each other on a perpetual basis—the stability thesis is a picture of the world that has been latterly overturned by scientific developments in post-Newtonian mechanics that concern relativity, contingency and decay.

Romanticism was concerned with nature, the seasons, emotion, power, affect, death and any intensification or heightening of the senses. However, we misunderstand the wide-ranging impact and importance of romanticism if we contrast it as being in opposition to, for example, the functional social sciences. One might be tempted to do so, due to the evolution in positivism in the social sciences that emerged largely after the work of Auguste Comte on positivism that was published in 1848[55]. Comte repudiated much of the previous work in romanticism in the social sciences, with his insistence on external empirical observation and the logical validity of systems built on reliable data sets. In contrast, romantic science had insisted on the unity of external empirical data and the potential internal maelstrom of the artist or seeker after knowledge. One of the most enduring examples of the romantic thesis and the unity of man and nature comes in the work of the philosopher, Friedrich Wilhelm Joseph Schelling, and his *Naturphilosophie*, which has recently come back into philosophical and intellectual focus after having received much ridicule and even having been dismissed as fanciful during and after Schelling's lifetime[56]. Schelling is credited with having come up with the modern notion of the unconscious, because his *Naturphilosophie* includes an intuitive, synthetic element which processes data imaginatively and allows for and explains the most extraordinary aspects of nature. Schelling was searching for an expanded realism that would not stifle the creative imagination, which he hypothesised had, for example, invented mythology. Indeed, Schelling went on to suggest that it was mythology that had conceived of the mind. Rather than keeping the fruits of the human mind such as mythology separate and away from natural science, Schelling looked for a means to meld nature with human thought, and in so doing to go beyond the dualism of the observer and observed in positivistic scientific method. Schelling also looked to philosophise beyond the idealisms of Kantian, Fichtean or Hegelian philosophies, which created internal engines of the human mind, and deflected or largely ignored the realities and chaos in nature. One could argue that Schelling's *Naturphilosophie* therefore functions on the level of a new materialism[57] which is able to explain the workings of nature without separation from the creativity and synthesis of the human mind, even though he characterised his philosophy as a form of objective idealism.

The danger with Schelling's *Naturphilosophie* and with romantic science in general is that it can create non-empirically verifiable objects. In contrast to a steam-engine, which can be designed according to thermodynamic principles, measured and latterly evaluated for efficiency, Schelling's philosophy creates a universe where 'unthinged' elements abound and which is backgrounded by 'unthought', a dark abyss or in 'the ungrounding'. One could say that Schelling's account of the world literally parallels a H.P. Lovecraft story, yet ironically, the latest discoveries in physics such as dark matter, the Higgs particle or Higgs Boson field closely resemble the world according to Schelling. The other compelling reason that Schelling's philosophy has come back into vogue after many years of obscurity is the search for a mode of thought capable of thinking through the consequences of the anthropocene. Human development since the time of the industrial revolution has garnered and encouraged its own systems, which have incorporated the thermo-mechanics of steam-power into the social organisation necessary for factory life and the prevailing economics of industrial production. Schelling's philosophy suggests a synthetic mode of thought that explains these elements of the anthropocene 'in-themselves' without diminishing their connective and destructive potential. For example, and as the Schelling scholar, Joseph Lawrence has said with respect to contemporary industrialisation: "The Earth does not have the carrying capacity for a universalized suburbia."[58] This statement is possible according to Schelling because we have the capacity to think through the consequences of a universal suburbia, and not due to the scientific means to verify such a statement quantitatively, which demonstrates a different set of thought processes. The tenets of immanent materialism point in a similar direction to that of Schelling in terms of understanding the spread and effects of suburbia, as we reconstruct the plane of 1815-1825 through this chapter, and the consequent dynamics of suburban emergence.

Another text that demonstrates the intellectual challenge to steam-power in the plateau of 1815-1825 is Mary Shelley's classic novel, *Frankenstein*. The central figure of *Frankenstein* is a scientist, who searches for the meaning of life by reanimating stitched together body parts and thereby creating 'his monster'. The scientist subsequently retreats from the reality of his creation and runs away from any responsibility to take care of it or to teach it how to live in the world. One can transcribe the romantic character of Victor Frankenstein from the Mary Shelley novel to James Watt, the production of the steam-engine and the construction of the 'life of the machine' through everything that has evolved around the steam-engine such as factories, industrial landscapes and economic development. Certainly, James Watt is not responsible for everything that has transpired since he worked on improving the efficiency of the steam-engine in the eighteenth century, yet one can by analogy with *Frankenstein* understand how the drive to efficiency, mechanisation and the calculation of energy inputs and outputs has migrated into aspects of everyday life such as the routines of the factory, education and thought. Mary Shelley paints an outside to the mechanised and repetitive production of thought, as the scientist of her story works through leaps of faith, creative inspiration, isolation from the mainstream, and the rejection of consolidated processes. Rather, he feverishly invents his monster, then, aghast at his creation, rejects wholesale what he has made and runs away. Likewise, James Watt and his contemporaries have put into motion a series of events that have resulted in the anthropocene, dangerous environmental change and the dominating mechanics of global capitalism. The point here is not to demonise James Watt by claiming that the calamites which have befallen the planet and the human race due to industrialisation are his fault, but to understand how the effects of steam-power are still operating. These effects are knowable, when, for example, as a global audience, we switch on and watch the royal wedding in 2011, and inter-connected, historic systems of conformity, work and thought click into place. I would like to explore these immanent material factors of the plateau of 1815-1825 through the metaphor from the Pink Floyd song: "Another brick in the wall".

"Another Brick in the Wall"

In the song, "Another brick in the wall", education is charac-terised as oppressive and soul-destroying, teachers are building divisive walls and the students are represented as bricks, pieces to be manipulated and put into place without care or attention for the individual's needs. In fact, the Pink Floyd song depicts education along the same lines as working in a factory, with meaningless, repetitive tasks producing alienation and derision in those who perform them. Certainly, from the perspective of immanent materialism of this book, the inspiration for the atmos-phere and grinding drudgery of "Another brick in the wall" comes from the plateau of 1815-1825, the migration from rural settings to the factories, and the ensuing continuum of lifestyles connected to the mechanisation of factory production. The steam-engine sits at the heart of the matrix of industrialisation, and forms a diagram that is a pervasive influence on society. Perhaps Pink Floyd could have merged the figure of the teacher with the influence of the new industrial machines and ways of life connected to factories more fully, so that the human outline of a teacher is blurred betwixt the mechanical parts of steam-power. The truth is that there was no mass education in Britain at the time of the industrial revolution between 1815-1825, so the immanent inter-relationships between factory life and education were not produced until after the Second World War in Britain and the education reforms of that period. In 1815-1825 the specific profession of being a teacher was restricted to a very limited number of medieval schools such as Eton College. The nineteenth-century proliferation of English public schools had not yet happened, rather, education for aristocrats and the wealthy most often took place in stately homes or in abbeys and churches. In other words, there was little connection between industrialisation and mass education at the time. Perhaps this is another reason why the transition to steam-run factories, capitalist surplus value creation and the social structure to make factories productive were successfully integrated, despite the agrarian and intellectual road blocks to the rise of steam-power. One could argue that people became 'bricks in the wall' because they knew little else—they could not think or do otherwise.

Of course, it is heavy-handed to brand whole populations in the same category or with a similar level of cognitive or reflective development. What is interesting from an immanent materialist perspective is how the life in the factories of the industrial revolution driven by steam-power has formed transversal connections with and in education over time. When Pink Floyd sung about 'another brick in the wall', they were referring to the ways in which industrial production has manifested itself in the production of individuals through schooling in England. In the UK, these processes describe a post-war landscape that had its beginnings in the plateau of 1815-1825 which is being analysed in this chapter. It is interesting to note that contemporary understanding of the nature of the mainstream teacher was absent from the initial construction of the plane, as teachers were not part of the industrialised landscape. Rather, teachers have been added to the ways of working in industrial contexts over time, and since the post-war education reforms have produced a mass education system that serves an industrialised population. The role of the teacher in an industrial context is therefore foregrounded by the work of the factory foreman, the factory floor supervisor and any other officials connected to the life of the factory, such as the production managers. These roles of the teacher necessitate that the formulation of multiple strategies for classroom management have come to predominate in many pedagogic contexts, and these strategies block examining the full processes of inter-mixing between populations, knowledge and knowledge use[59]. Teachers in urban districts are currently tasked with keeping students at their desks, making sure that they turn up and leave on time, and continually monitoring their productivity, however standardised or meaningless the output[60]. If all this wasn't enough, teachers are now expected to negotiate the changing landscape of post-industrial production, which includes the ways in which digitalisation has entered mainstream work processes, e.g. through office and computer tasks.

For these reasons, teachers are continually 'torn apart' by the plateau of 1815-1825. Teachers are backgrounded by the authoritarian figures necessary to keep factory production on track and are expected to be able to negotiate the changing modes of production in contemporary capitalism (see chapters 1 and 7). This expectation is an impossible task given the ways in which capitalism is accelerating and going beyond the previous formulations of its modes of operation and has incorporated feedback mechanisms through digital networks. The explosion in e-Business over the past two decades and the ways in which global capital flows are now able to be mobilised through the internet have taken the thermodynamic principles of steam-power to a whole new level. The figure of the authoritarian human teacher stands rather weakly and in contrast to the multifarious ways in which post-industrial capitalism is redefining, relocating and accelerating industrial production. Factory production of the kind emanating from 1815-1825 in the UK has largely migrated to cheap labour markets, post-industrial countries currently have to grapple with the new nature of production, international financial exchange, and the requisite training that should be attended to in order to equip the work-force with the necessary skills to negotiate the current state of global economic activity. Cognitive skills are clearly highly prized and should be taught, but what specific types of knowledge serve us in a changing and precarious global job market? These questions are perhaps too large for this book and the detailed analysis of the plateau of 1815-1825, yet they do relate to the next section of this chapter, which is to establish an immanent materialist connection with capitalised education.

The machine of 'capitalised education'

The capitalised education of this book is a machine—it has an input and an output, and a mechanism which transforms the energy relationship between the input and the output. The subject of this book, Kate Middleton (or KM, see chapter 7), went to the elite Marlborough College in England and St. Andrew's College in Scotland, where she met Prince William. One could say that the capital flows which have gone into creating and moulding Kate Middleton have precisely defined her current prestige and position in British society, and these flows depend on the mechanisms of capitalism and the ways in which capitalism has allowed for and augmented social change. One should not look for the origins of the type of social change as defined by Kate Middleton (KM), but one can examine the immanent materialism of these processes. This immanent materialism leads back to the period of 1815-1825 and the many ways in which the industrial revolution in Britain was changing society, as the new steam-machines introduced thermodynamic processes into factory, social and economic life. The period of 1815-1825 was a decade of great social change, and these changes have rocked the continued domination of the feudal system and the agrarian-aristocratic-state-religious complex that had ruled Britain previously. It is interesting to note that in the contemporary, globalised context, wherein macro-economic policy and social change are integrated on an international scale, the story of KM and her ability to rise from the middle to upper (royal) classes in Britain is almost a minor story. What is relevant and worth examining with respect to the capitalised education of KM is how a machine has evolved around such processes.

To understand this machine one must fill in the backstory of the plateau of 1815-1825, as well as analyse the contemporary situation (see chapters 1 and 7). At the heart of the backstory are the ways in which rural populations were attracted to the new working conditions, cities and lifestyles in the factories of the industrial revolution. These populations went from living close to nature and the natural seasons to living wholly unnaturally, or to being displaced from a natural existence. Furthermore, and co-existent with this change in focus and growth of the urbanised majority, was an understanding that these populations had to be kept in check and conform to the new modes of industrial production that were driven by steam-power, through contiguous developments in policing, state functioning, jails, marriage, urban churches, new tax regimes, rented accommodation, and public houses serving alcohol. Even though the rural populations who went to work in the factories did earn more money than their rural subsistence existences had previously allowed them to earn, their lives were little improved by the shift from farm labour to factory labour. The physical-mental machinery that the new urban poor were introduced to included shift work, endless repetitive tasks, and the social, cultural and imaginary ways in which they were regulated in their behaviours as factory workers and in the rest of their lives. This over-regulation resulted in a diminution of the ability to do or think otherwise, and this political and social effect has been passed on by generations who have lost any sense of place or connection with the land, and who have been thoroughly acculturated into the machine of industrial machinery both politically and personally. In contrast, the beneficiaries and owners of the factories, who were often the aristocratic owners of the land in the early nineteenth century, saw an unprecedented rise in their fortunes. Britain did not experience a widespread, internal, class-based revolution during the period of 1815-1825, as had happened in France (1789-1799), where the ruling aristocratic class were annihilated and their power was replaced by a republic. Rather, the differential power between those who controlled the means to production and those who enacted the means to production increased, as the surplus value of input versus output was expanded by steam-power. Crucially, and pivotally in terms of this book about Kate Middleton (KM) and her rise to contemporary prominence, reflection or any reflective practice was not inserted into the processes of industrial production of 1815-1825. The factories and social landscapes of the industrial revolution were machines that had no collective identity or self, they had no learning or adaptive capabilities, and were not reconciled as bodies or as having explicit inter-connections.

The immanent materialism of this book (re)designates the reflective aspects of industrial landscapes as one of their primary qualities. This means that the actual effects of factory living spreads out and interacts in other areas of life, such as the educative practice as described in this book, and in this chapter with specific reference to teachers. One may find parallels here in the work of Lewis Mumford, and especially in his notion of the 'megamachines', in which humans are inserted into the processes of larger machines as components. Teachers in modern industrial technocracies serve specific purposes that are pre-defined and rule out reflective singularity or the ability to truly think otherwise, for example, the ability to question the hegemony of the technocratic machines into which teachers are inserted through capitalism and bureaucracy. One of the fundamental purposes of this book is to open up this space, not in an agrarian or intellectually opposed manner to stream-power, but as systematic waves of reflectivity that sit conjointly with stream-power, or as 'the virtual' as Deleuze designates the thought processing of immanent materialism in a phrase he derived from Bergson[61]. The plateau of 1815-1825 is an important aspect of this process, because it contains the transitional and cross-over effects of the rural-urban complex, and is therefore a matrix whereby one might understand the expression 'becoming-machine' with respect to life in the factories and beyond. Yet the question of precisely where Kate Middleton (KM) fits into this matrix is necessarily open to speculation and interpretation (see chapter 7).

Kate Middleton's capitalised education is derived from the machinery of contemporary British capitalism as described in chapters 1, 2, 3, 4 and 7, and is a story of social climbing and opportunity based on being able to refine and redefine her background—including accent, smile, knowledge and poise—and to blend in with the established ruling aristocratic classes. However, the genesis of this specific rise in prestige and power comes from the industrial revolution of 1815-1825, and the manner in which the migration from subsistence rural life to entrenched laboured life opened up the possibility of access to capital flows through understanding the processes of production.

In exceptional cases, factory workers were able to ingratiate themselves so fully with the machine processes, that they could occupy increasingly important positions of power on the shop floor. Most of the land was still owned by the aristocrats and the Anglican Church, but non-aristocratic industrial owners did emerge from the nexus of 1815-1825, and these individuals and groups had the technical knowledge necessary for industrial production and commercial distribution of their products, combined with the ability to communicate with and manage the repetitive gestures of the majoritarian work-force in the factories. This is the backstory to the industrial revolution of 1815-1825 and the immanent aspect of the capitalised education of Kate Middleton. Kate's rise to prominence and her chances of success depended on the ways in which her path had been opened up and enhanced by successive flows of capital and capitalists through the UK's hierarchical class system, as social mobility was realigned and augmented by machine processes such as those pertaining to steam-power. The questions remain as to exactly how these processes worked, their real and imaginary effects, and whether one can fully place this backstory only in the UK, or if it has transnational or indeed global effects.

Global machines

There is much contemporary analysis of global capitalism, globalisation[62] and the transnational culture, society and habits that are embraced by and relate to these terms, for example, in the values personified by the McDonald's chain of fast food restaurants. With respect to our story about capitalised education and Kate Middleton (KM), the ways in which the machines involved in her creation have interconnected through globalisation has its genesis in the plateau of 1815-1825, and the industrial revolution in Britain. Yet the immanence of the procedure is universal and not particularly British, or attached to any nation state. Rather, the ways in which capitalism has evolved has always been necessarily global, yet often politicised, explained and demarcated as national, in order to hide the ways in which the pan-national economic system has exploited and dominated foreign lands in conjunction with military might and religious coercion. This cross-hatching of concern, desire and reality has been neatly expressed by the photo architectural blogger Christopher Schwartz[63] with respect to the notion of capitalist realism:

> It also has a totalizing tone, but somehow liberal at the same time, in a Hobbesian sense, of outward conformity that allows for inward or out-of-sight, out-of-the-way plurality—in other words, it doesn't matter what one does and desires "privately" (whatever *private* is in this context) so long as they do their job well, i.e., grease the wheels of commerce. The untenability of this position notwithstanding, the ideology at least purports not only to not want to invade one's innerspace, but it often claims that by allowing a certain degree of freedom and idiosyncrasy, the system as a whole can become stronger. After all, the heroes of capitalist realism, unlike the heroes of socialist realism, are the rogues, the mavericks, the outliers, the individuals.

This quote sums up what is at stake with respect to the immanent material analysis of capitalism, and in particular with respect to the acceleration, integration and functioning of machines in the 1815-1825 plateau. What happened was that the trade relationships that had been built up over three centuries by, for example, the East India Company, were suddenly more valuable. This is because the raw materials that could be sourced from the empire holdings in India and bought at unequal terms of trade prices, could be shipped back to the UK, processed in the new steam-powered factories, and redistributed as products throughout the empire at huge profits. Likewise, factories could be set up anywhere that used the new stream-based technology to make the production processes more efficient and precise. The continuity in interest and desire that was established by the new machines, steam-power and large scale factory production, can be summarised by understanding how profit margins work, and how unequal terms of trade had to be in place for these profits to be realised. These processes necessitated one side of the equation having inadequate or missing information about what happened during the various capitalist exchanges involving the production of products from the raw materials and the sale of these items. The victims of such a lack of information were the producers of the raw materials, often in the colonised lands such as India. The profiteers were the established aristocratic classes in Britain who had the capital to invest in industrialised ventures, and an emergent class of entrepreneurs, who are referred to as heroes in the quote from Christopher Schwartz above.

The global industrial machines therefore have their genesis in exploitation, misinformation and the establishment and masking of inequality. Such emergent qualities are clearly at odds with contemporary calls for social justice and redress with respect to centuries old unequal terms of trade between industrialised and non-industrialised countries, unfair labour conditions and any parallel social attitudes such as racism and discrimination. Yet such ideology is propounded and extended by contemporary commentators who want to leave decision making to the market, and the neoliberal *laissez faire* of capitalist realism. In contrast, this publication, by analysing beneath the skin of the contemporary situation, looks to unearth the complex entanglements in history that have gone to make up the capitalised education of Kate Middleton. The philosophy of 'immanent materialism' is important here, because such entanglement has an enormous projective and consummate power, in that the forms and forces of industrialisation have combined around the world and through time to make a new type of conformity that values profit margins, efficiency and the vertical divisions in labour above everything else. Such conformity can be explained by applying a philosophical approach which unravels the ways in which orthodoxy works, i.e. through belief, sentiment, irrationality, conditioning, the impossible, the unnerving and the invisible. The challenge therefore of this chapter and how the plateau of 1815-1825 fits in with the rest of the book, is to imagine the ways in which the morphogenesis of industrial landscapes has spread out and created global machines. One such osmotic effect and overriding concern, and perhaps the reason why rebellions against a capitalised education such as the Russian Revolution and the transformation of Nazi Germany have largely failed in Britain (see chapter 5), is because the previous widespread immanence of God has been replaced by the immanence of money[64].

Of course, there are still churches and congregations and belief in the divine as espoused from the pulpit. The argument here is that the ways in which the industrial revolution of 1815-1825 has spread out and formed complex interconnections on a global economic scale, has deep ramifications for thought and for the future. The acceleration inherent in industrial processes, and that is exemplified by the mechanics of steam-power, has derived and created new codes which we all now live by. In real terms, the organisational hold and drives of mainstream religion have been hollowed out and replaced by economics, and the ways in which habits that were previously dictated by going to church were latterly formed and determined by factory life. In urban British landscapes, the working day of the factories created routines and pathways wherein populations clocked in and clocked out, went home to spend time with their families and socialised at local public houses and perhaps in new urban churches. The real power of God was diminished from the rural location, where the populations had a closer contact with nature and therefore could be attuned to the mystery, wonder and transcendence of God. In their urban settings, driven by economics, repetitive factory work and the multiple enclosures of the new terraces, the populations were abstracted and displaced from close alignment with anything super-natural. Rather, urbanisation itself and the envelopment of machinery in all aspects of life have formed a new and monstrous reality that spread out and made global machines. These global machines have defined a horrific sense of otherness through time, which has been commented on and described since the plateau of 1815-1825, and is a vital substratum to the capitalised education of Kate Middleton (KM).

Horror, fear and the other

There is a well-known story, articulated by the likes of Edward Said and others, about the creation of the exotic 'excluded' other of the Orient, through the cultural, social and political workings of colonialism, the British Empire, racism and the formations that made up the mental-affective space of Britain in the nineteenth and twentieth centuries[65]. What has perhaps not been so well remarked upon is how this construction of the other started at home and in the factories of the industrial revolution. George Orwell and others have written about such matters[66], the analysis of this book adds to the descriptions and political analyses of socially aware critics, by identifying the inception of urban otherness in the factories of the 1815-1825 plateau. In fact, this otherness became pivotal to what could be understood by the term British in the nineteenth century, because Britain gained precedent as the industrialised heartland of the world during that period. The intensity and coverage of the industrial otherness was internalised by the population and carried on the numerous British trade routes by the ships of war and commerce that traversed the globe. What we find is an increasing abstraction and division of the self through the dynamic forces of production driven by steam-power, and this abstraction was occulted in terms such as 'the British' that became inter-changeable with 'the Colonial'. The British colonialist, as a repre-sentative of the forces of production that were immanent and real due to the influence of the domestic plateau of 1815-1825, primarily feared the horror of the industrial landscape from where they came from. All other fears, for example, of natives, savages, exoticism, blacks or women were pre-determined by the fear of the new industrial landscapes and the factory life that it had spawned. The adventurism and endless travel of the colonial were escape routes from the ultimate prison of the mind, the enclosures of endless factory life.

What we find, as we investigate and examine in detail the immanence of the 1815-1825 plateau, is an ever widening gap between the opportunities and life for those who could and those who could not take advantage of the British expansion and domination of world trade by the global machine of raw product inputs, industrialised process and profit from manufacturing outputs. This basic mechanism has not halted since that time, though the game is now a truly global and technologically complex and accelerated one, and cannot be reconciled with any one nation or country state. If one takes the situation in China today as being analogous with Britain in the nineteenth century, the same internal divisions and tensions are prescient. The problem for the ruling Communist Party in China today is that they cannot effectively raise the standard of living for the majority of factory workers without ruining their low-cost manufacturing labour base. The inevitable effect of this tension over time will be mass protests, strikes and industrial action on an ever increasing scale. Meanwhile, the influence of China throughout the world will continue to grow as they search for partners to supply raw materials to feed the existence of the uneasy life in the factories. However, the overall effect of the life of the factories in China is a brutal reality of pollution, social unrest, conformity to the rules of production and a belittling of anything that potentially steps in the way of progress such as free speech. Britain in the nineteenth century followed a similar path, which ultimately led to the dismantling of the British Empire and the contemporary shrinkage of British industry in terms of dominating world markets other than perhaps those involved with finance and English teaching.

The question of what is real became an important one for the colonialist, as they went around the world with the otherness of factory industrialisation buried within as a type of perturbation. The question of what is real is co-existent with, who am I? and what will I become? Alongside these questions are the fear of the loss of rationality, a fear of the loss of the self and control, and the fear of what is not-real. The development of these fears and otherness as a consequence of the plateau of 1815-1825 and the industrial revolution, results in a break and interruption in learning about the world and the impossibility of complete realism. For the colonialist, it was impossible to fully appreciate what he or she was experiencing as the otherness of British industrial production gnawed at their consciousness and revealed troubling dreams. The phantoms of the realities of industrial production in Britain were continually at the back to the British explorers' minds, however much they tried to ignore them, or created illusionary realities in their new locations. In Australia, this movement of British thought, based on the horror, fear and otherness of the 1815-1825 plateau culminated in the declaration of a white utopia through Federation in 1901. The new society in Australia was to be built on egalitarian grounds amongst the white settlers and descendants of the convicts, yet almost entirely ignored the rights and thought processes of the Aboriginal people, and any heritage that excluded the thorough-going industrialisation of life. In contrast, the Aboriginal people, as Inga Clendinnen has commented:

"They [...] developed steepling thought-structures – intellectual edifices so comprehensive that every creature and plant had its place within it. They travelled light, but they were walking atlases, and walking encyclopedias of natural history. [...] Detailed observations of nature were elevated into drama by the development of multiple and multi-level narratives: narratives which made the intricate relationships between these observed phenomena memorable.[67]

The immanence of the British invasion was of industrialisation, extermination, racism, discrimination and class. The immanence of the Aboriginal people, that was largely overridden, subjugated or ignored by the British, was, as the quote from Inga Clendinnen suggests, of a completely different nature and order. It is in this context that we speak of a need for a different epistemology and ontology with respect to, for example, the learning needs of Australia children, a learning that takes seriously the heritage of the Aboriginal peoples and creates a space where the outlook of the Aboriginal people is taught in schools. The current curricula and knowledge structures in Australia still almost entirely favour the British invaders, and carry with them the immanence of the plateau of 1815-1825. The horror, fear and otherness that has been perpetrated on the Aboriginal people carries on through the schooling and learning processes in Australia, even though there have been attempts to sincerely apologise to the Aboriginal peoples for past wrongs by, for example, the Australia parliament in 2008. The point here is that the immanence of industrial processes, dating back to the 1815-1825 plateau, still has an impact today, and are prolonged by the forms of life that have inherited the characteristics of factory existence. When television audiences in Australia react to and evince emotions such as pride and nostalgia whilst regarding news about Kate Middleton, they are, in part, summoning the buried sentiments from the plateau in this chapter. In many respects, life in Australia still follows a factory model of thought that intuitively despises intellectualism, is sceptical with respect to other cultures and lacks any spirituality. Of course, one cannot absolutely generalise about such matters, though the construction of this plateau, which represents a crucial period in the beginnings of the white Australian nation, does point to a nexus and crossing-point in terms of what Australia has to overcome in order to move on from the past. White Australia lacks any history prior to the convergence between industrial production and commercial gain during the period of 1815-1825, and this immanent influence to a capitalised education shall be explored in chapter 6. The thought of feudalism is only present in contemporary Australia as a dream or love of Europe, and as an imagined connection to the royal family of Britain, viewed with reverence and fake pageantry during television events such as the Royal Wedding of 2011.

Conclusion

The 10 years of this plateau are crucial in our understanding of KM as media object and a capitalised education, because this plateau works as a crucible and springboard for integrated world capitalism. This is not a statement of empirical historicity, but part of the immanent material analysis of this book. Indeed, for those living through this turbulent period of British history, the events and themes that run through this chapter must have felt very different from the establishment of an empire. In the contemporary situation, the British nature of the set-up of integrated world capitalism has all but been lost, as countries around the world have latched onto and exploited the systems and modes of working that were invented in the UK. For example, in the USA and China, the forms of capitalism that have latterly emerged have taken the intensities from the plateau of 1815-1825 and up-scaled these convergences to their precise contextual and demographic needs. One of the interesting aspects of this immanent material analysis of KM as media object and a capitalised education is that KM has been able to penetrate and flourish given the current nature of international world capitalism. Perhaps the legacy of the British Empire and the use of English as a *lingua franca* have helped KM as media object in her progression towards world domination, her image and style are readily translatable into different cultures. The important point to take forward from this chapter is the momentum and power of technological development from 1815-1825, and how this energy seeps into every other plateaux except chapter 6, which comes before the inventions of Watt had occurred.

Chapter 5

Political responses to a 'capitalised education':

i) Lenin, Russia 1917; ii) Hitler, Germany 1933

Introduction

One of the major problems that we have in understanding the 'capitalised education' of Kate Middleton as an influential whole or as a specific phenomenon, is that the processes and systems that it represents have been previously undefined and have escaped specific scrutiny by folding into 'the natural order of things', 'the way things are', or, perhaps worse, Kate Middleton's capitalised education could be perceived as an instinctual expression of social progress and success. The contra argument to the immanent material thesis of this book is summarised in that we would all follow in Kate's footsteps if only we could, that there is no politics attached to a 'capitalised education', that her progress has in fact been value neutral. This book argues to the contrary, and that an inter-mixture of subtle and complicated political and historical manoeuvrings is involved with and unearthed by the immanent material exploration of a 'capitalised education'. A way into explaining this point is through under-standing the immanence of political systems which have deliberately moved outside of a 'capitalised education', and can therefore effectively isolate and shine light on the thought of a capitalised education. One such system is represented by the Bolsheviks of the Russian Revolution in 1917, another by the National Socialism of the Nazi Party in Germany, 1933. These revolutions in Russia and Germany demonstrate alterative political and social systems and inhabit different yet comple-mentary plateaux, as shall be analysed in this chapter. Deleuze and Guattari date one of their *1000 Plateaus* as 1933, and called it 'Micropolitics and Segmentarity'. This chapter follows many of the points originally made by Deleuze and Guattari with respect to this plateau, and expands upon them in terms of their relationships with a 'capitalised education'. Félix Guattari wrote a paper in 1971 called, 'The Leninist Breakthrough'[68] in which he analysed the happenings of 1917 in Russia, and developed a Lacanian approach to understanding how the subject could be structurally co-opted into revolutionary action through language, a point which has latterly been expanded and reinforced through the work of Slavoj Žižek[69]. Both Guattari and Žižek focus upon Lenin's April theses, in which he declared the Bolsheviks should immediately seize power. However, Guattari came to change his approach to Lenin through his writings with Deleuze on 'Capitalism and Schizophrenia' and in his later book called *Molecular Revolutions* (1977). The perspective that will be taken forward in this chapter is the material semiotics of the later Guattari and Deleuze and Guattari, and not the Lacanian treatment of linguistic subjectification to the April theses. Material semiotics works both in the situation of Russia in 1917 and in Germany 1933, because the specific historical and political conditions allowed for and created the possibility of the messages of Lenin and Hitler to become incorporated into variant political assemblages and decisively into the becoming-revolutionary of the situation[70]. This chapter deals with the dual processes of the Russian and Nazi revolutions from a material-semiotic perspective that throws light on a 'capitalised education', and examines how societal power was seized from the bottom-up, until it oozed and flowed through the new cultural formations of communism and fascism.

Lenin-the-man

The cult and personality of Vladimir Ilyich Lenin is still powerful today by dint of the combination of his actions and his words. It is almost inconceivable that any contemporary political leader could produce the voluminous writings that Lenin was able to execute as well as take over and subsequently run a country. Lenin stands out as an enormous personality, 'a man' who could get hard political changes done, as well as being able to explain what these changes were about. For most of us, the thought of taking over, reconstructing and maintaining a social-political-cultural system would be daunting enough, without the added burden of producing a coherent political commentary and theory on everything that he accomplished. These dual truths about Lenin point to the fact that he was tremendously literate, articulate and decisive, and especially with respect to the application of Marxist theory in life. The main aim of Lenin and the Bolshevik revolutionaries was the overthrow of the tsarist hierarchical system, which was still rooted in feudalism and Christian mysticism, even though the technology of nineteenth-century industrialisation had begun to seep into many aspects of Russian society. The defeat of capitalism was meaningful to the revolutionaries in that the capitalised-aristocratic classes held the means to production, the land and the money. Lenin had been working assiduously to raise the levels of class consciousness amongst the proletariat since at least 1887, by getting involved with illegal revolutionary parties and publishing banned revolutionary material in any way that was possible. By 1917, the specific ground had been laid for the final and ultimately successful revolution across the vast expanse of urban and rural Russia. Lenin had been in exile for much of the twentieth century before the events of the 1917 revolution, except for a brief period during the unsuccessful 1905 revolution, and in that time he had been able to publish revolutionary works, organise meetings, and plot the overthrow of the tsarist regime. In his time away from Russia, Lenin saw the point of the revolution not only to improve the material lives of the majority of people in Russia, but to mark a turning point in world history. According to Lenin, the revolution in Russia would serve as a model for further Marxist revolutions, and the over-turning of imperialist political-social systems around the world. The point of this immanent material analysis is therefore two-fold, firstly to understand how and why Lenin succeeded in his crusade to change the system in Russia, and why further revolutions did not immediately happen as a consequence of the events of 1917 in Russia.

Lenin did not act alone, but was aided by like-minded revolutionaries such as Stalin and Trotsky, all of whom had had to work illegally to promote the revolution. One could argue that organising anything collectively which is illegal is galvanising, especially if the revolutionaries were sent to prison together as happened, or were able to meet in exile in order to communicate and finalise their plans from afar. The illegality of the revolution is why one sees multiple and generalised modes of development around new forms of communication, before and during the Russian Revolution. The revolutionaries had to innovate, codify and covertly disperse their forms of communication in order not to get caught by the imperial authorities. The political pamphlet was sliced with and in daily newspapers, the newsletter changed form and gained immediacy and potency as a communiqué, local news took the form of ideological brochures and revolutionary tactical analysis, in fact, any means that could carry the messages of imminent social change to the desired audience, i.e., the proletariat, was used by the revolutionaries. Lenin wrote a text called "On Slogans" in 1917, in which he declared "All power to the Soviets" and through which he invented a new, politicised class of workers, who were told to unite: i.e., "Workers of the world, unite!" One may ask the questions: Who precisely were the workers? How could they unite? What did uniting mean in real terms? What did they have to gain from uniting? The revolutionary communication machinery was working in overdrive before and during 1917 and the answers to these questions were already becoming apparent to the majority of the population in

Russia. They—the majority—were the workers, and uniting meant social change in terms of overhauling the increasingly defunct and old fashioned tsarist system. The use of revolutionary messages had convinced many in the population that the social change to come would benefit them. Yet why were Lenin and his allies believed by the majority? How did the population in Russia know that the new communist system which was being proposed by Lenin would work any better than the existing imperial tsarist system, which had been aligned to Orthodox Russian Christianity and the form of Western capitalism as analysed in chapters 3 and 4? The truth was that the majority of the Russian population did not know that communism as a social system would work any better than 'imperial-capitalism', yet the multiple lines of communication that had been established, and the determination and the fervour of the Marxist revolutionaries, had captured the imaginations of many Russians before and during the conflict of 1917, i.e. "What could happen" had become a ubiquitous thought in Russia, and this thought was, in the end, powerful enough to win the day.

The Russian Revolution was ultimately successful because the Bolsheviks had turned the minds of many military men in their favour, and a proportion of the existing military fell behind and fought for the 1917 revolution. Some may argue that the events of 1917 in Russia were a *de facto* civil war fought between royalist and anti-royalist forces. This statement is true to a certain extent, yet the difference in terms of the immanent material analysis here is 'Lenin-the-man', the new system of communism that subsequently resulted in Russia and what these phenomena represent with respect to a 'capitalised education'. The Bolsheviks did take power by force, and they had to consequently fight a civil war against the counter-revolutionaries, the White Russians, who opposed Lenin and the Bolsheviks. These violent actions of Lenin and his henchmen became known as the 'Red Terror' because of the ruthless ways in which the opponents of the new Soviet Republic were dealt with at the time. Yet this is not the place to moralise against the actions of Lenin, the plateau of 'Lenin-the-man' and 1917 is immanent to the contemporary situation to the extent that one may learn how to enact social change. For example, the varying distances that Lenin was able to create between himself and revolutionary action on the ground in Russia is an important factor in social change. Lenin was like a force of nature with respect to the political and social situation of the period, seemingly emerging from outside of Russia to help change the material conditions inside of Russia, rather than being universally seen as an activist or politician who had worked tirelessly on the inside to make change happen. The fact that Lenin came from the outside of Russia gave him extra momentum and scope for change. His subsequent appearance in Russia was exciting and new, he was different, 'an exceptional other' who was suddenly in the midst and at the heart of the revolution which he latterly came to personify. Lenin's distinctive 'Tartar' looks helped to consolidate this image of exciting otherness and difference.

Lenin took on and exemplified the forces of social change in terms of his character and his will to make the changes in the Russian social system binding and permanent. By eliminating the power of the ruling aristocratic classes, Lenin freed up movement in Russian society for a time, and launched a new wave of Marxist-Leninist aspirational talk, action and social clamouring. The problem for Lenin was not so much the taking of power as it happened in 1917, as what to do with power when it had been taken. One could say that the resulting Marxist-Leninism from 1917 became a Russian orthodoxy, and when the transfer of power from the tsarist-imperialist state to the communist state had been completed by the 1920s, the paranoid over-coding of the totalitarian state system became apparent, and led to the establishment of the secret police, who enforced the orthodoxy of the state by torture, punishment and brain-washing. Certainly,

'Lenin-the-man' made the revolution happen, and for a time the continued success and expansion of the revolution was his most consuming desire and thought. However, he was unable to ever completely dismantle the apparatus of the tsarist-imperialist system, despite early democratic advances in terms of the establishment of a myriad of functioning worker committees, state run farm communes and legislative organisations for workers to contribute to and enter into genuine debate about their positions. Yet the apparatus of state oppression was still operant in Russia after the revolution, and many in the new communist political leadership fitted into the skeletal remains of the apparatus, even with the new access routes to the workings of power from the bottom up that were introduced by Lenin and the Bolsheviks. Other countries did not immediately take on the mantle of the Russian Revolution, even though the influence of Lenin in 1917, has been felt throughout the world ever since. Countries such as the USA became stubbornly anti-communist after 1917, and identified more deeply with capitalism as the nineteenth century progressed, partly as a result of making everything connected to the Marxist revolution 'the enemy of freedom'. Russia and the greater Soviet Union became more isolated and closed to the outside capitalist world as the twentieth century deepened, and resulting power abuses in such a system were inevitable, yet from the plateau of Lenin, 1917, the totalitarianism of the decadent Soviet Union was not imaginable. What had been achieved in 1917 by the Bolsheviks and by Lenin was a complete Marxist revolution and the death of organised religion.

Rasputin the Anti-Christ

One of the primary targets for elimination by the Marxist revolutionaries and Lenin was the Orthodox Russian Church. This was because the Marxism of the new system was a materialist ideology that opposed the mysticism of the church. Lenin and the Bolsheviks promoted the scientific investigation of the world in unison with a social system that used the fruits of science to help the majority of the population. One of the reasons that the specific combination of science and Marxist social change was successful in Russia in 1917, was because the mystic, Grigori Rasputin, had infiltrated the Russian royal household due to his apparent healing abilities with respect to the sickly heir to the throne, Tsarevich Alexei. Rasputin had the reputation of being a sexual predator, alcoholic and fraudulent holy man, and this reputation was widely known across Russia. Lenin and the Marxist revolutionaries seized upon the position of Rasputin as an example of the decadence of the Russian royal family—to them, Rasputin demonstrated the mystical ways in which the royal head of the state operated, without any real care or under-standing for the general population. The political line of argument that the Bolsheviks focused on depended on two widely recognised weak aspects of the royal family, their hered-itary illnesses, mainly haemophilia, and the reliance on mystical advisors that can be associated with the workings of weak, unfocused minds. In contrast, the Bolsheviks were extremely focused on the goal of social Marxist revolution and had no hereditary, mystical or blood filiations. The main reason that the Bolsheviks had become grouped together, and worked effectively as a united front, was due to their absolute opposition to and hatred of the existing Russian imperial regime, and their common interest in Marxism as revolutionary politics. If one takes away from a political situation any talk or action associated with aristocratic blood lines, or that comes about due to the importance of heritage, or that involves the value of social division by classes and the positioning of the aristocrats and their immediate associates at the top of the social ladder that had been in place for over a thousand years; one is left with a political vacuum that is filled by the emergence of the new Marxist revolu-tionaries. One of the ways in which this enormous and relatively fast over-turning of social norms was successfully achieved was through the figure of Rasputin.

For many of the religiously inclined rural dwellers in Russia at the time, the association of Rasputin with the Tsar must have been extraordinary. Such an unholy alliance would have seemed to them as if the devil himself had crept into a position of influence in the parlours of power in the Russian royal establishment. Rasputin's actions and personality created rumour, scandal and allegations about everything that he came across and touched, and such was the outcry that his assassination by those who wanted to protect the monarchy in 1916 was inevitable. Hereafter, it was an easy job for the Bolshevik revolutionaries who were working to overthrow the monarchy to focus on the existence and influence of Rasputin as a political weak point in the royalist arguments. The existence of an infamous 'Anti-Christ' in the midst of the political intrigues of the times was a gift for those looking to sway the minds of the peasant and working peoples across the nation, who only had access to rumours and gossip. The facts of the matter were less relevant than the reputation that Rasputin had managed to engender for himself, and the damage which this reputation could do to support for the monarchy across Russia. In contrast, the revolutionary Bolsheviks suggested practical and concrete ways to improve the lives of the workers, they were not steeped in mysticism or fraud, and had a plan to rationalise and update the workings of the general economy. The important point here for the 'capitalised education' of Kate Middleton and the immanence of the plane of Lenin, 1917, is that Rasputin is a sort of political black hole or strange attractor, which draws in other opinions, actions and forces that fall within its remit. This black hole gnawed at the continued existence of the royal family in Russia, and became more powerful than a thousand years of heritage and power. Rasputin represents a tipping point in the history of Russia and an immanent reason for the destruction of the monarchy. This immanence is still relevant today, even though most royal families have been extraordinarily careful not to be associated with mystics since Rasputin. However, royal lineages across Europe include the genetic weaknesses introduced into the bodies of the aristocrats by the restricted blood lines and the in-breeding programme of the upper classes across the centuries. Genetic weakness is another reason that the outsider, Kate Middleton, is so important to the royal family of Britain, as she introduces genetic diversity into their limited gene pool.

One could argue that the forced death of the Orthodox Russian Church by the revolutionary Bolsheviks and Lenin in 1917, created the conditions for a type of transference effect, wherein the rituals, habits and beliefs of Christianity were trans-ferred to the learning, practising and dissemination of Leninist-Marxism. In other words, in Russia, the Bible became *Das Kapital*, the liturgy of the church was transformed into the regulations and requirements of workers' meetings, and the Eucharist was reinvented in terms of connecting to the inner sanctum of the 'politburo'. On one level, this transference effect is a distortion of real history that explains how people carried on with their lives after such major social upheaval as the events of 1917, without entering into the complex local networks and relationality that has to be undone and reformed for anything to happen or change. On another level, the transference effect tells us about the factors of succession in the new Soviet Union, through which priests were replaced, churches were reused or destroyed and the congregations of local communities were dispersed and reassigned on different paths. What is interesting from an immanent materialist perspective is what happened to the belief in God in Russia after the revolution, and what replaced the need for a belief in God as a worldview and comforting presence. The plane of revolutionary action and thought that is attached to Lenin, 1917, saw an upsurge in the study of the sciences, and the social sciences took precedence in the attempt to build a coherent and well founded Soviet Union. Most of these social sciences were connected to the use of Leninist-Marxism philosophy in the building and maintenance of the Soviet Union in the twentieth century and are therefore redundant in the current situation, however, one aspect of these social sciences has burgeoned and expanded since the end of the Soviet Union, and that is the ideas connected with the Vygotsky Circle.

The Vygotsky Circle

One of the main challenges to understanding the significance of the Lenin, 1917, plane of immanence today, requires the demonstration of how communities around Russia learnt to do things differently under communism. Arguments against communism contend that many communities across the vast expanse of Russia carried on with their traditional ways after 1917, ignored the dictates of the Leninist-Marxism state, until they were perhaps visited and impelled to change their habits by a Bolshevik party member or the military. The problem, therefore, of the Lenin, 1917 plateau in terms of immanent materialism, lies in understanding how to bridge the gap between a naturalistic approach to social behaviour and learning, and one which is defined in advance by a philosophy such as Leninist-Marxism. One answer to this problem is through the teaching and learning of Marxism and Leninism at school as an explanatory frame for social behaviour, yet the danger with this approach is that Leninism and Marxism could become uncritical dogmas for school children, even when incorporating critical questioning into the ways that they work. The social sciences in the Soviet Union after Lenin, 1917, had to directly grapple with such a dilemma. The demonization of capitalism and imperialism in the USSR, and the closure of links between the USSR and the West, made contact and inter-communication between scientists in the Soviet Union and the non-communist world impossible. However, the study of social behaviour started afresh in the Soviet Union, and was energised by the new materialist philosophy that had been determined for the system by Lenin and the Bolsheviks. The Vygotsky Circle of related scientists working with the ideas of a young Lev Vygotsky developed in the USSR as a consequence of revived interest and investment in scientific explanation of social behaviour and as a push to use this knowledge in education.

The story of the emergence of the ideas of the Vygotsky Circle into the mainstream of Western educational thought is an interesting testament to the ways in which the plateau of Lenin, 1917 is immanent now. The learning ideas of the Circle were largely ignored until a newly revised and compiled, international version of their earlier scientific work was published in 1961. Social and educational scientists in the USA and elsewhere were looking for new paradigms to explain social behaviour in the 1960s, and the freshly edited views of the Vygotsky Circle fitted in with this desire[71]. The tenets of Leninist-Marxism were largely eliminated in the take up by Western social scientists of the ideas of the Vygotsky Circle, and, for example, the ZPD (Zone of Proximal Development) and scaffolding became incorporated over time into the Western educational canon without regard for the conditions of emergence of the theories or their immanence. In other words, Western educational practice and theory incorporated the notions of scaffolding and the ZPD in countries such as the USA and elsewhere without the prior social revolution. Henceforth, the ideas of the Vygotsky Circle were isolated in the West in terms of being an educational methodology to enhance social learning and were simultaneously disconnected from politics, philosophy or economics. In many ways, the revolutionary potential of the Vygotsky Circle's ideas were neutralised because the extraction of the ZPD and scaffolding from the general work of the Vygotsky Circle came without context[72]. The influence of Vygotsky on Western education persists today as a means to enhance educational practice or as a 'how to', but is entirely disconnected with any notion of what to teach or why to teach. The use of the ideas of the Vygotsky Circle in education has been incorporated into a general theoretical practical move, stemming from the public education of the 1960s in the UK and elsewhere and that merges the social constructivism from Dewey and a child centred education.

The child centred, constructivist educational movement of the West should be viewed positively, as the child is now usefully endowed with agency in this equation, and the child's progress is repositioned as being at the centre of the knowledge construction that happens in the classroom. However, such a form of educational humanism does not define what should or should not be taught in the classroom, and has no defence against invasive neoliberalism to move in and take charge of the educative political arena in terms of market normativity and learning reproductivity. One could state that extremely wealthy private schools and poverty stricken state funded schools can equally implement scaffolding and the rebadged notion of the ZPD in their classrooms to enhance the learning outcomes of the students, yet this learning enhancement will not start a socialist revolution or deal with entrenched social and cultural inequity. Ironically, the idea of an education revolution has recently reappeared in Australia in terms of introducing new 'Information and Communications Technology' (ICT) based teaching and learning tools by the Labor government of Kevin Rudd in 2010, which in a parallel manner to scaffolding and the ZPD, sought to accelerate the potential of students to learn, without defining what should be learnt or the social purposes of these ICT mediated learning objects and lessons. One could say that it was therefore an easy gambit for commercial providers and profiteers to move in and supply the new ICT teaching and learning hardware and software, without providing the under-standing that attention should be drawn to what the students will learn and the social purposes of this learning. In contrast, this chapter, which is analysing the plateau of Lenin, 1917, recognises that learning is not neutral, but carries with it sometimes deeply buried social-cultural and political messages. The schools in Australia that have received the new ICT installations have put them to very different purposes. The elite private schools used the ICT to teach and learn about the ways in which to enable their students to access the global jobs market, where people are mobile and work for companies and governments around the world as specialist, highly qualified professionals. The financially strapped state schools generally used the equipment to make existing lessons more interesting through flash, ICT mediated audio and visual resources, which they hope might quell some of the classroom management issues and make lessons more engaging. A true education revolution in Australia would give every child from whatever background the same expectations in terms of job and life prospects and have the material means to deliver this vision.

The plateau of Lenin, 1917 represents an invigorating and important experience of social change and of "what can happen". For those of us experiencing mounting regimes of debt as students or citizens in the midst of the financialisation of society, and the inevitability of further and more intractable financial crises to trouble us in the future as capitalist life accelerates without remit, the plateau of Lenin, 1917, is a particularly attractive and powerful force of immanence. This plateau directly cuts across the 'capitalised education' of Kate Middleton because the political assertions of Leninist-Marxism seriously question the continued material importance and power of the aristocracy. Defenders of the royal family in Britain might point to the value of 'royal-tourism' (however, do the royals need to be kept alive for this?), or the direct and indirect economic benefits of harbouring and servicing the royal cohort, or even the social benefits in terms of consistency of having a social system defined by a stable, hierarchical aristocracy and the resulting class snobbery. In conclusion, the material analysis of the 1917, Lenin, plane of immanence presented here does not brow-beat or preach one 'correct' view on the matter of the royals and social revolution—you—the reader, must decide for yourself and take steps to address the 'capitalised education' of Kate Middleton once you have understood what is possible and what is the right course of future action.

Adolf Hitler

Perhaps the darker side of this plateau, but one which is equally as immanent and relevant to today's situation, is that represented by Adolf Hitler in 1933. As the world of present day capitalist endeavour plunges into a potential abyss of financial crisis, environmental catastrophe and international social upheaval, echoes of Hitler, 1933 resonate around the globe as right-wing politicians gain support and feed off the fears of the majority. Hitler, 1933 has a very real importance to these politicians as a model and a method for the means to seize power. In contrast to Lenin in Russia in 1917, who focused on the material conditions whereby people lived, Hitler worked on unconscious emotion, on instinct and on the herd mentality of those who listened to his words and those who read his ideas in *Mein Kampf*. Lenin's was a planned and coordinated material revolution that expunged Russia of the aristocracy and attempted to eradicate the whole imperial edifice which supported the regime of the Tsar, Hitler's rise to power was a sustained and conscious attempt to link politics with the occult. Theoretically, the Nazi Party, with Hitler at its head, had associated their ideas with those of Friedrich Nietzsche and, in particular, with the unpublished notes contained in *The Will to Power*[73]. Hitler's speeches and ideology were designed to create the conditions whereby the will of the German people could be unified and joined in triumphant emergence. Yet in practice this objective was achieved not through reading, analysing and acting on Nietzsche's ideas, but on the collective mobilisation of racial categories and the spread of generalised hatred and fear towards the Jewish people and other marginalised groups on the grounds of racial purification. Rather than challenging the continued existence and material importance of the ruling aristocracy as had Lenin, Hitler and his Nazi ideology preserved the German aristocratic heritage and class as a symbolic order and as added weight to his argument about the racial superiority of the German race, while at the same time replacing their power and influence with that of the Nazi Party. Hitler, Germany, 1933, therefore will represent a very different political response to the capitalised education of Kate Middleton than Lenin in Russia in 1917.

Lenin's response to the capitalised education of Kate Middleton would be to dismantle the aristocratic groundings and structures upon which it rests through revolutionary means. Hitler would preserve the mythological, symbolic and ritualised groundings of the capitalised education and realign them under the Nazi ideological machine and functioning of the fascist state. Under Hitler then, one would therefore experience an augmentation of the effects of the capitalised education of Kate Middleton as symbolic, but not real power and not a diminution, extinguishing and redistribution of the influence of imperialism on a practical and molecular level, as would happen under Lenin. Hitler's energetic defence and consolidation of his position in 1933 saw his rapid rise to a position of power and eventual influence over the whole of the German system as chancellor of the Weimar Republic. Unlike Lenin, whose Bolshevik Party remained illegal until it had forcefully taken and consolidated power after 1917, Hitler and the Nazis used the existing political structures in Germany, and went from an illegal fringe party in the 1920s to the only legitimate political organisation in 1933 and 1934. Hitler paid his respect publically to President von Hindenburgh as an outward sign of his loyalty to the leader of Germany in 1933, but immediately moved to remove the presidency from the legislature of the Weimar Republic after

Hindenburgh died in 1934. In effect, Hitler and his Nazi Party took over every vestige of power during 1933 and satisfied their collective will to power in 1934. Once they had taken over, they forcefully repressed and suppressed any opposition by violent and ideological means, including the construction and use of concentration camps, as well as the organisation of new symbolic rituals that were meant to solidify and enhance the power of the Nazis in the minds of the general population. In contrast to Lenin, 1917, the plateau of Hitler, 1933, produces a notion of power that works in and through itself on every level, and not for the purposes of a social revolution or the material betterment of the population. Yet the becoming-revolutionary of the Hitler, 1933 plateau is powerful and immanent, as, for example, the recent resurgence of right-wing politics in Europe has demonstrated. The immanence of Hitler, 1933 comes about because there were always the underlying concerns for death and glory in their plan and which was an integrated and essential part of the Nazi Party program as Deleuze and Guattari describe:

> Fascism, [in contrast to totalitarianism], involves a war machine. When fascism builds itself a totalitarian State, it is not in the sense of a State army taking power, but of a war machine taking over the State.... in fascism, the State is far less totalitarian than it is *suicidal*. There is in fascism a realised nihilism[74].

Swastikas and the death-drive

The political immanence of Lenin, 1917 is to make a better social system, to overturn the injustices of the past, and to address contemporary issues of inequality that may delay progress towards communism. In contrast, the immanence of Hitler, 1933, revolves around the ways in which the social system can be reworked and remade to serve one principal cause, that of sacrifice for the greater German nation or any other national cause. Yet if one reads the speeches of Hitler in 1933, one is struck by how coherent, forceful, rational and persuasive they are, how communism is cast as the force for death, and how the new Nazi order is described in the most positive terms as a means to gain the full employment and success of the German people.[75] Hitler and his speech writers were able to mask the reality of their suicidal and nihilistic program behind the rhetoric necessary to convince the population that they were the guarantors of the German people (*das Volk*) for the future. In many ways, the immanence of the conjunction Hitler, 1933, is the most slippery and deceptive of all the plateaus of this book. On one side of the political equation, the Nazi push to absolute power by any means defined a pragmatic and unprecedented use of the irrational drives and all existing power structures in terms of subordinating language, thought and emotion to one cause. On the other side, this subjectification by any means to the Nazi program, cause and supposed ultimate triumph, annihilated all possible moral hindrances to reaching this goal. The concentration camps, fear tactics and extermination of any opposition was folded into the will to power of the Nazis through the grand delusionary strategies of the Hitler war machine. Hitler's absolute conviction in the Nazi cause and the ways in which the Party were able to incorporate signs and symbols such as the swastika into the accumulative death-drive of fascism proved to be the decisive factor in terms of understanding how power was gained and consolidated through Hitler, 1933.

The semiotics of the combined swastikas and Hitlerian death-drive were the means whereby the Nazi Party controlled the masses. The majority of the population were forced to wonder whether the Nazi Party, with the absolute conviction politician, Adolf Hitler, at its head, and with an abundance of signs such as the swastika emerging in its wake, didn't have a claim to legitimacy after all. The death-drive was hidden as a suicidal machine, racial purification and the possibility of the greater

Germany, yet the energy which this machine was creating was obvious, as the motivational aspects of the drive rippled through the population. People didn't exactly know that they were enacting Hitler's death-drive when they signed up for road construction projects, worked in the munitions factories or participated in Nazi Party events. What the population felt was a conviction and drive that had been lacking beforehand under the politically liberal or social democrat regimes. As with the Lenin, 1917 plateau and the communist revolution, the middle ground of politics had been taken away, the recourse to dialogue or a multi-party system was denied, the social system was reprogrammed and restructured from the inside according to Nazi strictures. Germany was sent on a new trajectory in 1933, as was Russia in 1917, and both of these social-political paths were no longer subject to the normative oscillations of a multi-party system in a neoliberal democracy which tends to protect market economics. This is why real political and social change happened according to the Lenin, 1917 and Hitler, 1933 plateaux, and this change was absorbed and redefined by the resulting communist and fascist state systems. Communism in 1920s Russia tended towards totalitarianism, fascism in 1930s Germany tended towards self-destruction, even though the 1930s Nazi Party could be understood in terms of emergence and power expansion.

The utopian expectation of a functioning communist state is still immanent today as a result of the Lenin, 1917 plateau and the intention to make social-cultural life more equitable. The dystopian trajectory of a Hitler, 1933 fascist state is immanent in that the amalgamated conditions of financial crisis, environmental catastrophe, global terrorism and continued human population growth make the takeover of a state system somewhere in the world by a far right political party inevitable. Certainly, one is not left with a simple either or between communism or fascism in terms of the politics of the future, yet these two systems do present themselves as immanent and relevant options, as the world teeters on the brink of inter-related systems collapse. The continued neoliberal political promulgation of free market economics under a one world capitalist system has resulted in enormous economic injustice and the continued existence of aristocratic class dynamics as represented by the capitalised education of Kate Middleton. One of the points of this book is to construct an immanent material response to the politics of the future and to understand how one can imagine a new political dimension which avoids the oscillations of extremism in communism (as totalitarianism) or fascism (as the death-drive), and does not uncritically reproduce the politics of neoliberal free market economics. Recent interest in accelerationist politics is one possible avenue to explore in this regard, as has been suggested:

> The future needs to be constructed. It has been demolished by neoliberal capitalism and reduced to a cut-price promise of greater inequality, conflict, and chaos. This collapse in the idea of the future is symptomatic of the regressive historical status of our age, rather than, as cynics across the political spectrum would have us believe, a sign of sceptical maturity. What accelerationism pushes towards is a future that is more modern – an alternative modernity that neoliberalism is inherently unable to generate. The future must be cracked open once again, unfastening our horizons towards the universal possibilities of the Outside.[76]

Currently, the accelerationist movement is confined to a pressure group on the internet, yet given the conditions of non-linear change that are upon us due to climate catastrophe, financial instability and capitalist inequity, perhaps the accelerationist movement will gain momentum as the twenty-first century progresses. The point here is that the semiotics and immanence of swastikas and the death-drive of the Nazi Party state, or the revolutionary class-consciousness of Lenin and the Bolsheviks, have been superseded by the financialisation of the neoliberal state, which incorporates the realities of boom and crisis as has been demonstrated throughout capitalist history (see chapter 7). Accelerationists suggest that the only way out of these boom and bust cycles is to accelerate them and at the same time to engineer a generalised flattening of capital flow, similar in kind to some highly technologized societies, which heavily regulate the markets through taxation such as in Finland and Norway. Perhaps the greatest danger to the continued stable existence of the Scandinavian state countries is the re-emergence of the Hitler, 1933 plateau, but in the form of reactionary Scandinavian right-wing extremism. The racial purification argument is still raised in the European north as a response to immigration and changes to the demographics of Europe from the south in terms of Islamification that is already affecting parts of Scandinavia. One could perhaps figure the future of politics in terms of assemblages—one based around the Lenin, 1917 plateau, another around the Hitler, 1933, and the middle ground being populated by numerous political options and assemblages that always tend towards the neoliberalism of free market capitalism. Acclerationism appears as a new political form in this middle ground, one that avoids the oscillation and drives of the extreme left (totalitarianism) or the extreme right (swastikas and the death-drive), and at the same time makes one aware of the failures of the present neoliberal market system. The point of this immanent material analysis and political plateau of Lenin, 1917 and Hitler, 1933, is to understand how a politics of the future may be constructed that moves away from the capitalised education of Kate Middleton without being reduced to neoliberal republicanism, or any other market based political option that exacerbates inequity. This idea is comprehensible by positing a relationship between a capitalised education and the notion of 'the pack'.

The return of the pack

The effects of the stylised and grand return to neo-pagan blood ritual and occultist ideological thought control through the positing of one cause, i.e. sacrifice for a greater Germany by the Nazi Party, was an attempt to return to a pre-modern pack. The Nazi Party organised a generalised feedback system whereby state policy and functioning directly addressed the unconscious drives. The population was reanimated and motivated to join the packs; for example, one sees in Nazi Germany a return to metaphors of collective hunting and a ubiquity of focusing on the enemy within or weakness, whether it is due to genetic impurity or a lack of commitment to the German cause on the part of the agent. The pack mentality of the Nazis was an externalising force that left nothing on the inside, and as has been argued ultimately leads to death and therefore unearths and utilises the death-drive as an extra supplement of non-moral energy. The war machine gathers around and through the pack and organises the life of the pack without the formal restraints of the state system either as internally imposed boundaries or as externally determined limits; i.e. the pack ultimately heads towards and locates death through mobilisation and flexible movement. This is one of the prime reasons that the plateau of Hitler, 1933 is immanent to today's situation and to the political landscape in which we find ourselves enmeshed. For example, many right-wing groups in the USA today identify with a broadly anti-state and anti-government agenda, because they want to distance themselves from any association with the Lenin, 1917 plateau and a state controlled society. In essence, the right-wing advocates want to return to the perceived freedoms of the pack, and away from the bureaucratic controls of a state run society, which heaps regulations, limits and directives on the small holder or 'little guy'. This is also the point that one may become confused by the precise politics of Deleuze and Guattari and the immanent materialism of this book, as the nomadic pack is advanced by them in positive terms.

Deleuze and Guattari do not advocate a straightforward anti-state or anti-government political position as has been articulated by some Tea Party members and political commentators in the USA, or a return to fascism. Deleuze and Guattari critique the totalitarian state that resulted from the Lenin, 1917 plateau, as an example of paranoid over-coding, in, for example, the deployment of the secret police and rigidity of the Soviet communist state apparatuses. The nomadic pack and war machine of Deleuze and Guattari emphasises the sedentary social and spatial arrangements that can be inherent in state procedure. Deleuze and Guattari speak about royal science as being associated epistemologically and ontologically with the sedentary and control-driven aspects of the state, and these connections take one back to the capitalised education of Kate Middleton. Kate has had to learn about the physics of distance that properly pertains to her new role in the royal family of Britain. She has had to reengineer herself as someone who can simultaneously act like a royal, i.e., aloof and apart from the mob, yet remain personable and project a positive media image. The point here is that Deleuze and Guattari's nomadic politics forces one to ask questions about the sedentary nature of the state and the politics that reinforces this position fixing and accumulative set of actions and directives[77]. Kate's capitalised education is a process that can politically fix us into place as an attitude and an audience for the contemporary adventures of the young royals. The processes and politics of a capitalised education are, of course, reinforced by the existing class system of the UK, and the historical divisions between the classes and the ways in which these divisions have been reinforced, for example, through royal control of the state system, the law and through personal and collective factors such as memory (see chapter 6). The inertia, immutability and transcendent nature of the state that has produced the capitalised education of Kate

Middleton are the targets of the critique by the nomadic politics of Deleuze and Guattari, through the designation of micro political war machines or packs.

The result of the designation of war machines to undermine the capitalised education of Kate Middleton is a matter for speculation. For example, Eugene Holland, a respected Deleuze and Guattari commentator, has spoken about a slow motion revolution, an adaptive and environmentally responsible process of social change that incorporates the latest technology and processes of democracy to rebuild and enhance society for the future. As a vital element of this social change, a major problem is represented by eliminating oil and coal as power sources for the future in that oil and coal are globally the current most cost effective means to produce power. Consequently, the nomadic politics and pack mentality of immanent materialism targets the reliance on globally orchestrated market economics as a controlling factor in the way in which power is produced by unravelling the assemblages involved with market economics. The idea is not to replace the existing state systems with the fascism of swastikas and the death-drive, but to use the current systems to channel the energies of the pack into responsible social change of the type that Holland advocates. Holland speaks of nomadic citizenship, through which the lifestyles, attitudes and choices of the environmentally responsive nomads are fed into large scale society and its organisation. Rather than the accumulation based, sedentary culture which is dominated by the signs of contemporary global capitalism, Holland foresees a system of semiotics and exchange based on environmental responsiveness, 'living in nature' and with nature and not solely through capital[78]. Perhaps this approach has swallowed some of the romantic connection with nature that the vitalism and Spinozism of the Deleuze and Guattari project can tend towards, yet in the face of imminent climate collapse one cannot help but to be swayed somewhat by such an approach[79]. Yet one must also return to the present to construct the immanent material plane through which the Hitler, 1933 plateau works.

The reality of the present political situation is that oil and coal production and their use is backed up and continues because of lobbying and pressure from multifarious business interests which currently make enormous profits from their integrated systematic uptake through capitalism. To change this entrenched system requires the pack to fundamentally address the ways in which the use of coal and oil are currently integral parts of advanced industrial countries. Such a push to change requires scientific investigation into carbon neutral power sources, carbon sequestration, and the integration and implementation of these new power systems globally. In this way, the nomadic pack of Deleuze and Guattari can be set up and pushed in an opposite direction to the plateau of Hitler, 1933. The Hitler, 1933 plateau redesignated and redefined a new 'fascist science', wherein cross-, inter-, and trans-disciplinary investigations worked towards the upholding and promulgation of the fascist state. In the current situation, the notion of a nomad science works to produce similarly integrated studies that tend towards a wholly different goal, that of an environmentally sustainable future and an increased democratic involvement in this future. The resultant vestiges of the state, regulation and the law, and the usefulness of the figures such as Kate Middleton, the royal family of Britain and the 'capitalised education', should be judged in the light of these future goals.

Conclusion

The politics of a 'capitalised education' is exposed and challenged by this combined plateau, which has considered the immanent material effects of Lenin and Hitler. However, one should not figure the politics of a capitalised education as inhabiting a middle ground between polarised and polarising opposites. Challenging the political forces and groupings behind

KM as media object, means understanding how they influence and work together to change opinion and alter the affective atmospheres within which KM as media object is embedded. For example, the commercial interests in KM as media object are concerned with the ability of her image to sell items such as clothing and magazines. This book advocates a critical approach and resistance to the connectivity between KM as media object and the commercial interests that benefit from her ideal presentment. Yet this criticality is sieved through the lens of immanent materialism, which adduces the immanence of KM as media object and a capitalised education and follows the material flows that work through such immanence. Therefore, the criticality that one might want to take from this text with respect to KM as media object is expanded and reflexively softened, until this movement of thought allows one to examine everyday life (human and non-human). However, in order to fully appreciate the immanent material analysis of KM as media object a capitalised education and the politics which KM as media object entails, one needs a truly historical and mythological backdrop to the study, which examines many of the invisible ways in which KM as media object and a capitalised education function, and shows how KM as media object and its necessary learnings are embedded in entangled, power-related matters through time.

Chapter 6

Cynicism and heartbreak—the mythological backdrop to a 'capitalised education':

Henry II and Lady Eleanor—1150-1200

Introduction

The most historically based plateau with respect to this analysis of the immanent materialism of Kate Middleton concerns 'Henry the II and Lady Eleanor, 1150-1200'. The British royal family are able to convolutedly trace their blood lineage back to this first Plantagenet king and his impressive wife, who was a European aristocratic power broker in her own right. The historical details about this plateau, as can be understood from the records and the myths that have grown around the facts of the period, make the plateau of Henry the II and Lady Eleanor, 1150-1200, foundational to many of the ways in which one can understand the immanent materialism of Kate Middleton today. This foundationalism has come about because the facts and myths about the royal family are interchangeably linked into the ways in which the Windsor collective currently rule Britain and any remnants of the British Empire. The privilege, power, capital and immanence of the group of individuals who have landed in their positions through 'birth right', aristocratic lineage and the various apparatuses that have grown around and protected the royal family through history, are dependent upon the ways in which the general population views the foundations of their rights and lineage. These foundations concern the imaginative and affective means through which the royal family rule the country and beyond, in addition to the physical establishment and maintenance of a loyal military, parliament and church. These means involve the ceremonial, ritualised and coded forms of control that the royal family has used to suppress rebellion in the minds of the population. The work of immanent materialism is to uncover and analyse these forms of control, in order to bring us closer to the layered but real ways in which the royal family continue to exercise power, despite the potential anachronism of their continued influence. The set up and origin of the power of the royals is relevant today to the extent that these systems of influence are still operational. This plateau is therefore far from a historical recreation of a bygone medieval age, and is intimately linked to the ways in which the symbolic and material forms of royal power still hold sway.

The backdrop to this chapter paints an emotional landscape of cynicism and heartbreak. Perhaps one could crudely divide this emotional register, between Henry, who cynically managed his reign, increased his dominion and power at any cost, went to war with his foes and imprisoned his wife, and Lady Eleanor, whose Aquitaine court at Poitiers has become associated with the chivalrous romanticism of the medieval age. One could understand such a stark division between the influences of Henry and Eleanor as a matrix which touches us today when we consider the continued power of the aristocracy. On one side of the equation is a concern for absolute power, dominion, and property and in today's environment, the manipulation of capital flows, which one may associate with cynicism, on the other side is a concern for beauty, aloofness, aesthetics, love and religion, affect and the formal mannerisms of living an absolutely privileged existence, which one may figure through heartbreak. This chapter does not value or privilege one side of the matrix over the other, but looks to explore these influences from a balanced and immanent perspective that exposes and explores further knowledge with respect to the capitalised education of Kate Middleton.

The common law

Henry II's greatest achievement during his reign of 1154-1189 is considered by many historians to be the establishment of the 'common law'. The common law is the system of justice used in Britain and in many ex-colonial countries whereby judgements are handed down by courts which use the principle of precedent to assess the nature and seriousness of offences. Importantly, the judges and juries in the courts which employ common law are ultimately accountable to the reigning monarch. The relationship between the actions of the courts and the king was formalised and enacted by Henry the II, who built upon the system of law that had been put into place by his grandfather, Henry the I and the previous Anglo-Saxon kings. Henry the II had to overturn the power of the regional barons in Britain and France and the influence of the Catholic Church, who had taken advantage of the years of political instability that immediately preceded the reign of Henry the II and have become known as 'the Anarchy'[80]. Henry the II made all legal and property disputes in his domain accountable to the Crown, and thus gained control of the monies which were paid to the courts by litigants and the convicted, and thus dramatically improved the revenue stream of the monarchy and gained increased influence and presence in every corner of his kingdom[81]. Many consider Henry the II's system of common law to be the beginnings of the mediaeval state that was controlled by the monarchy, and which still remains in part today, and that ties economic, legal and constitutional power together under the name of the king or queen. To fortify the power of the state and the monarchy, Henry had to defend his continuing rule against the warring barons in England and France, the king of France and the influence of the Roman Catholic Church. The establishment and provision of the common law was a critical manoeuvre to achieve this goal.

The common law therefore emerges out of a feudal maelstrom of violence and vested interests. The immanence of the common law resides in such an atmosphere, which ultimately pertains to the maintenance of the British monarchy, even though the direct physical threat of being deposed has been largely removed through the legislative procedures of parliament and the House of Lords. The effects of the common law are fear and submission, which are reinforced through the ritualised procedures, archaic dress codes and ceremonies that surround the enactment of the common law in the justice system. One could perhaps cogently argue that having such a mechanism of reinforcement to the law, which could be understood as a form of transcendence with respect to the king or queen as a sovereign figure is largely positive, in that rulings are given gravitas and weight, in other words, there is a definitive ultimate linkage with sovereign power that resides with any judge or sitting court under common law. The problem with the workings of common law and the way that the monarch became the juridical head of the mediaeval state resides in what Giorgio Agamben has termed the 'state of exception'[82] and which Agamben took from his analysis of the work of Carl Schmitt. The state of exception is characterised as when a state is involved with a civil war and legal procedures are disrupted or ignored due to internal conflicts that have arisen in the ruling classes. Henry the II's compulsion to institute the common law across his realm came about due to 'the Anarchy' that had developed between his uncle King Stephen of Blois and his mother the Empress Matilda. The development of common law was a legal and juridical innovation that was an attempt to bring stability and peace to the 'state of exception' or the civil war that France and England had been engaged in between 1137-1153.

Agamben's study shows how the 'states of exception' became formalised and enshrined as necessities in the statute books of the legislative bodies of the state. Take, for example, the anti-terrorist laws that are increasingly encroaching on our civil liberties in terms of the right of surveillance by the state. In the case of the common law, the ways in which it was designed to maintain the monarch as the ultimate arbiter of justice and the majority holder of territory in the realm, that became known simply as 'the Crown', shows how the power of the monarchy works. Over time, the concept of 'the Crown' was disassociated from the actual body of the king, and became a ubiquitous marker of legislative power and influence, perhaps as Henry had initially desired. The mediaeval state, with its multifarious workings, territories, formalities, laws and holdings became progressively enmeshed in the web of what might be termed as 'the Crown'[83]. The power of the Crown therefore expanded and broached every aspect of life in the realm, with an actual power base in the mechanisms and revenue of the mediaeval state of feudalism. The continuing civil wars in Britain and France, which lasted for over 500 years after Henry the II had instituted the common law, have added impetus and penetration to the 'state of exception' and therefore to the power of the state over its subjects. The power of the monarch over the state has changed in form over time, yet there remains a strong and real attachment between the state and the Crown in Britain, and which should be considered in terms of the analysis of the capitalised education of Kate Middleton. The immanent materialism of this plateau and in particular, the power of the Crown over the state and the subjects of the state refers to the ways in which the set-up of the common law by Henry the II still constrains and guides the citizens who live through its edicts. The state no longer deploys capital punishment, so one could argue that the monarch currently does not have the power of life and death over its subjects. However, the present system of fines, prison sentences and the keeping of a criminal record by the state, acts as a mode of punitive connectivity between the Crown and the individual. Any action that might be classified under the common law as illegal could be prosecuted by the Crown, and hence one's actions are determined in advance by what has been documented in the common law and in the parliamentary statute books.

The system of the common law acts as a pivot to demonstrate and determine the power of the monarch within the mediaeval state. If the system functions well, revenue flows and justice is dispensed by judges and juries that serve the purposes of the Crown. In times of civil war, or where there is corruption or rebellion in the system, the role of the juridical power of the monarchy is altered and a 'state of exception' has to be declared to redefine the behaviour of the anti-royalist rebels as illegal. This action was usually performed through the passing of parliamentary or constitutional laws related to sedition and treason, and backed up by military or police means, as happened against the Russian revolutionaries who wanted to topple the Tsar. Agamben's point is that these 'states of exception' have become the norm, and in today's environment the state works through states of exception as a routine aspect of the legislative process, building in flexibility and ways of working that circumvent many of the safeguards that have protected citizens in the past. For example, any labour laws or protection for those gaining the lowest of wages are under constant attack from neoliberal politicians wishing to make all law subject to the rules of the market. Deregulatory laws expose workers to the excesses of the profit motive, or in trying to create products for the least amount of expenditure. Whilst industrial laws are not part of the criminal code or canon of common law, they do show how the state can intervene to affect the lives of the majority. With the monarch as ceremonial head of parliament, the statute laws passed by a representative body will align with the necessities of the royals, especially if the government of the day is a conservative one. The point here is to assess the immanence of the plane of 1150-1200, and Henry the II's legal framework remains an active part of the way the state works today, even given that the constitutional powers of the monarchy have been reduced over time by the parliament. A different aspect of the immanence of this plateau of 1150-1200 lies in the specific influence of Lady Eleanor, both real and imaginary, and how this influence relates to the capitalised education of Kate Middleton.

All you need is love

On the opposing but non-dualistic side of the plateau of 1150-1200, sits the influence of Lady Eleanor, and her so called 'Court of Love' at Poitiers in the south-west of France. Henry the II and Lady Eleanor had a tempestuous relationship, which began as a power marriage to gain territory and royal influence and ended in full scale war and Eleanor's imprisonment. The mythology about the 'Court of Love' at Poitiers has come about due to Eleanor's patronage of literary figures such as Wace, Benoît de Sainte-Maure, and Bernart de Ventadorn. In *The Art of Courtly Love*, Andreas Capellanus (Andrew the chaplain) refers to the court of Poitiers[84]. He claims that Eleanor, her daughter Marie, Ermengarde, Viscountess of Narbonne, and Isabelle of Flanders would sit and listen to the arguments of lovers and act as a jury to the questions of the court that turned around acts of romantic love. The chaplain records some twenty-one cases, the most famous of them being a query posed to the women about whether or not true love can persist in marriage. According to Capellanus, the women decided that it was not at all likely. However, Capellanus's account of the Court of Love is the only record that historians have of such events, and as such the existence of the 'Court of Love' has been disputed by historians, who require more concrete evidence for the court. In terms of the plateau of 1150-1220 and any immanent material effects, the 'Court of Love' is part of the combined influence of the roman-ticism of mediaeval literature and the ways in which the life and heritage of the aristocratic courts has been mythologised. This romanticism is connected to notions of chivalry, troubadours and courtly love, which define and exemplify a set of manners and rules for the expression and control of aristocratic social life. In more general terms, such notions of how the aristocrats should act have become imbricated with the aristocracy themselves, the Christian values of grace and the having of a generous and noble demeanour.

In Europe, perhaps the greatest and most powerful mytho-logical set of ideas associated with the romanticism of the 'Court of Love' is the legend of King Arthur. The first complete record of the King Arthur narrative comes from 1138, 30 years before the 'Court of Love' in Poitiers with Eleanor, and was written by Geoffrey of Monmouth as part of his imaginative history of British Kings[85]. The expanded legend of King Arthur gives us an originative myth about the mis-en-scène of the English Crown, as well as setting out the rules and manners of the knights, and exploring relationships between the knights, their motivations such as the quest for the Holy Grail and love interests such as that between Lancelot and Guinevere. The story that Geoffrey wrote focused on Arthur and his conquests as a successful warrior, and not the romantic aspects of the story, which were emphasised in the twelfth- and thirteenth-century continental versions of the Arthurian legend. Historians believe that Geoffrey pieced together the story of King Arthur from earlier fragments about a sixth-century Romano-Celtic King of Wales who had fought off the attacks of the Anglo-Saxons and had established an independent realm of Britain. However, there is no historical evidence for this character of Arthur, only the narrative as depicted by Geoffrey, fragmentary mentions of Arthur in Welsh poems and several earlier histories of Britain, and later, the proliferation of variations on the Arthurian romantic themes in continental Europe. The great revival in Arthurian legend came about during the height of the British Empire, as represented by Chapter 3 of this book, and which required a hero at the begin-nings of the British Empire to found a nation and to justify its considerable conquests and holdings in terms of an original, heroic and royal heritage. The imaginative recreation of Arthur, his knights of the roundtable and the adventures in the realm of Camelot in the Victorian age has added weight and immanence to the plateau of 1150-1200, precisely because these figures and their stories are widely recognised and repeated today. The retellings of the Arthurian legends have coincided and merged with Lady Eleanor's 'Court of Love' at Poitiers as a combinational part of the romantic mythology of what it means to be aristocratic and how one should behave in the 'upper classes'.

The immanence of the romantic notions of what it means to be part of high society still holds us transfixed as we watch images of contemporary royal pageantry or think about the existing hierarchies in society. The traces of these '1150-1200' plateau processes take their places in opinions and attitudes to the lowly, those who one might consider as being without manners or determined as 'the vulgar' or 'the uncouth'. One could say that the 'Court of Love' at Poitiers and the romantic notions of knights and ladies that we have today works from within to produce ideals and dreams of a bygone mediaeval era of social etiquette and rigid class structure. However, there is another aspect to the plateau and the projection of the 'Court of Love' into manners and social etiquette, which is mentioned by Deleuze and Guattari in *1000 Plateaus*. One can reconcile this different aspect of the plateau as a form of erotics that one may derive from the manuals on mediaeval love such as the one written by Andreas Capellanus. The abstraction of social life away from the everyday routines of habit, work and drudgery, transforms the notion of courtly love into a 'thing-in-itself', a self-fulfilling prophesy, at once an object of fascination and intrigue and a subjective inclination and strengthening of affect. Deleuze and Guattari relate courtly love to the construction of one's body-without-organs or BwO, which signifies an increase in intensity and a plane for the exchange and enunciation of desires that is wholly other to capitalist exchange. One could argue this conception of courtly love depends upon the concrete political and social formation of feudalism, wherein the majority of the population were locked into the lives and routines of peasants and servants. Yet this fact of mediaeval life is not the point that Deleuze and Guattari are making, the argument in *1000 Plateaus* is that the manuals of courtly love which were about the very upper classes, give us a clue how to live with resistance to the constraints of contemporary capitalism[86].

Writers such as Stendhal and Georges Bataille have investigated the idea that courtly love can be used as a means to strengthen subjectivity through the mechanics of eroticism[87]. The song, "All you need is love" came out of the late 1960s rebellion against mainstream Western society, which saw a separation between those who rejected military interventionism such as that exercised by the USA in Vietnam, and those who saw the military power of the USA and other allied countries such as the UK and Australia as part of an international police force that was safeguarding peace in the world. Such a separation in opinion is still prevalent today and highlighted by supporters and detractors of organisations such as Wikileaks. The immanence of "All you need is love" lay in the ways in which the song communicated a message that connected with an audience that didn't want to go to war. However, the interconnections between war and the global economy are deep and complex—those who didn't want to go to war and listened enthusiastically to, "All you need is love" frequently didn't want their economies to fail and therefore were living through a contradiction between their revulsion of war and destruction, and the maintenance of a stable, bourgeois lifestyle that depended on overseas military intervention. The connection between "All you need is love" and Eleanor's 'Court of Love' at Poitiers is that both serve to strengthen subjectivity, even if the 'Court of Love' at Poitiers is in fact a romantic invention, the notion of courtly love is a powerful one with a strong, immanent relevance. However, this notion of courtly love that we derive from the plateau of 1150-1200 should be differentiated from Christian love, which was an important part of the Christian message and the immanence of '1150-1200'.

Thomas à Becket

One wonders how priests could legitimately preach the notion of Christian love from the pulpit during the time of this chapter, 1150-1200, given the widespread and ingrained state of war. This period includes one of the most famous episodes in English history, when the Archbishop of Canterbury, Thomas à Becket was murdered in Canterbury cathedral by henchmen of Henry the II on Christmas Day in 1170. Becket was almost immediately canonised by the Pope at the time, Alexander the III, which was one of the factors that started off a long running dispute between the Roman Catholic Church and consecutive British monarchs. This dispute was not resolved until Henry the VIII moved to separate the British state from Catholicism and set up the Church of England in 1534. The dispute with Becket had begun with Henry the II and the reforms of the common law. The church had its own ecclesiastical system of law, which excluded priests or church officials from being tried by the royal courts of Henry the II. One could say that the Catholic Church had its own religious state system with its own courts, taxes and an enormous power base in Europe that led back to Rome and the Pope. Henry the II had tried to challenge the hegemony of the Catholic state system through the establishment of the common law and its requisite power structures, which brought him into conflict with Thomas à Becket who defended the existing power of the church. The Christian expression of 'Love thy neighbour' is a maxim that does not apply to Thomas à Becket and Henry the II at the time; however, more vital to understanding the plateau of 1150-1200, is the power structuring that both represent in terms of the formations of the mediaeval state.

Giorgio Agamben has investigated this issue from the

perspective of the apparatus or *dispotif*[88]. Foucault was concerned with the ways in which the state or 'governmentality' captures subjectivity through the individuation of rights and the ideals of the Enlightenment with respect to knowledge. Thus, there is, according to Foucault, an inbuilt set of strategies that one might understand as an apparatus or *dispotif* that traps and determines the relationships between citizens due to the administration of the state. Foucault worked as a detailed historian, who examined historical records to illuminate the idea of the apparatus, showing how power, knowledge, discourse and subjectivity function, with respect to, for example, prisons and madness. Agamben goes back further in time than Foucault and looks at the early theological use of the Greek term, *oikonomia*. *Oikonomia* was introduced into Christian theology from the previous Greek usage, where *oiko* had meant home, and *oikonomia* had designated the management of the home, found, for example, in Aristotle in terms of praxis. The early Christian theologians expanded the notion of *oikonomia* to refer to a general or divine economy, which was meant to describe and encapsulate the management of God's realm. However, a crucial division between the father, the son and the Holy Ghost was introduced into the notion of the divine economy by the church, whereby the praxis of the divine economy was regulated by the son, Christ, who became the absolute figurehead of the Catholic Church on Earth. One might perhaps cynically link the divine economy or *oikonomia* to the various income streams of the Catholic Church, and refer to Christ as the first CEO of Catholicism Inc. with the cross as the logo. The father (God) and Holy Spirit are less relevant to this economic set up than Christ, the economy of the church relies on the subjective worship of Christ by Christians and payments dependent on this subjective inclination.

Henry the II was a Christian, yet his apparatus of common law came into conflict with the apparatus of the ecclesiastical law in terms of income flows and juridical power. The solution to the problem of having two competing states in the same country was solved by Henry the VIII nearly four hundred years later, which worked by absorbing the revenue streams of the church into the state ruled by the monarch, and was unimaginable to Henry the II. He could not make himself the head of the church without risking war with the Papacy, and every other country in Europe that backed the Catholic Church at the time. Rather, he looked to appease the Catholic Church after Becket had been murdered and was raised to the status of a saint by the Pope, whilst still manoeuvring to make his common law effective and maximising its influence over his realm. Yet the murder of Thomas à Becket by Henry the II's henchmen marked the beginnings of the separation between the secular and religious state. Henry the VIII's solution of the problem as to who has the ultimate authority over the state by making himself the *de facto* Pope of England in 1534 was a long-term solution, and another stage in the movement towards separation of state and religion. One could argue from today's perspective that it should have been inconceivable that Henry the VIII had the ecclesiastical authority to run the affairs of the church, yet this change in leadership of the church has led over time to the Church in England having diminished power, that saw in government, for example, the appointment of chancellors being wholly secular. The Church of England retained land and revenue flows from their congregations, but their power never rivalled the influence of the mediaeval Catholic Church other than as a backup and spiritual reserve to the commercial and military exploits of the British Empire (see chapter 3).

Over time, the apparatus of the secular state has come to dominate the workings of the religious state in Britain, in contrast to Rome, where the Papacy still wields enormous, immanent, power. In countries such as Ireland and Australia, the conflict between the legal systems of the religious and secular states has recently been reignited with respect to the prosecution of paedophile priests, who had previously escaped prosecution precisely due to the remaining protections of ecclesiastical law, dating back to when the Catholic Church ran its court system internally. The immanence that we can take forward with respect to the capitalised education of Kate Middleton refers to these continuing fault-lines in the law and the processes of the law that surround their administration. Nowadays, with the preponderance of secular administration, bureaucracy and the interconnected systems of the state, the ways in which the established church retains its grip on power is often muted and hidden within the establishment of, for example, the monarchy. The monarch is the head of the church in the UK, yet this is fundamentally a ceremonial role, the power that the monarchy holds is in association with and because of its relationships with the government and the military. The immanent materialism of the monarchy is therefore down to the historical links between the monarchy and the parliament, which commenced in earnest after the reign of Henry the II in the thirteenth and fourteenth centuries. With respect to the death of Thomas à Becket and the relationship with the church, the assimilation of the Church of England by the monarchy over six centuries has led to a decline in the power of the church in Britain. However, one could argue that the Anglican Church has recently been able to reverse some of these historical losses at the hands of the monarchy largely by copying the tactics of the Catholic Church and moving into developing countries in Africa and Asia. Such an analysis would, however, take us away from understanding the capitalised education of Kate Middleton in relation to the plateau of 1150-1200. One aspect of the plateau that should be analysed and taken forwards in terms of the immanent materialism of today is the issue of gender and Lady Eleanor's role in the power manoeuvring of the time.

Gender wars

One could characterise the plateau of 1150-1200 as embodying an aspect of the gender wars which have been analysed and described in terms of feminist theory since the 1960s. Lady Eleanor was an heiress, and possessed some of the richest lands in Europe that were contained in the holdings of the Kingdom of Aquitaine. She was therefore a highly desirable bride and was married to King Louis VII of France for 15 years before this marriage was annulled and she wed Henry of Anjou who became Henry the II of England. The true character of Eleanor comes through the historical records and the accounts of the various royal courts of the time. One could perhaps further define her character through the ways in which France is itself divided between the cold north and the warm south. Eleanor comes across as a woman who was confident in herself, not as a vassal to the king, but as a ruler and monarch in her own right, warm and able to express and enjoy herself without having to ask permission. Later in her marriage to Henry the II, Eleanor sided with her son Henry (who later died) in open revolt against the king, she was imprisoned, and after Henry the II had died, she ruled England for 10 years in the name of her son, Richard the I, who went on crusades during much of his rule. Eleanor had been described at the time as beautiful; she must also have been in command of a powerful character and strong will-power to succeed during the period of 1150-1200, where power was often defined by the actions of the sword. Eleanor has left a mark on culture and history, and not as a shadow of the king, but as a figure in her own right, who didn't let gender get in the way of retaining power.

One can only speculate how exactly Eleanor maintained her control and power during the period of 1150-1200, despite, for example, the fact that her husband had many well publicised affairs, one even resulting in a son who she cared for at their palace in London. One could argue that Eleanor's education, which is described as being of the highest quality, contributed to her self-assuredness and ability to retain a regal position amongst Europe's elite of the time. Furthermore, the fact that she was already an important heiress before she was married to the king of France and the king of England, certainly provided Eleanor with a formidable mantel in terms of being considered as an equal or superior to her husband kings. As a woman, Eleanor was vulnerable to kidnapping and armed male attack, and usually had a protective brigade of soldiers at her disposal, especially when travelling across Europe. What matters here is the type of knowledge or epistemological base that one derives from Eleanor and the plateau of '1150-1200', and the resulting ontology or nature of being and becoming one might want to induce with respect to the capitalised education of Kate Middleton. Kate appears content at the moment not to question her role as wife of the heir to the throne, unlike her predecessor, Lady Diana (see chapter 1), who gave an interview at the end of her marriage that detailed exactly what had been taking place between herself and the Prince of Wales, Charles. The Duchess of Cambridge seems unwilling to critically or publically analyse the situation in the royal household, and would rather play the role of a dutiful wife and new member of the royal family. Kate has fitted in with a corporate perspective on the royal family, as shall be analysed further in chapter 7, and has added her positive media image to the outward aspect of the royals without providing any critique or analysis of its systems and functions. In contrast, Lady Eleanor took on the power of her husband and the power of his state system to an extent through her bravado, free-will and partly through her considerable resources as the Duchess of Aquitaine. The most immanent aspect of her actions that we have today is that the best way the royal family can be challenged and divided is from within.

Contemporary feminists have questioned the veracity of epistemological and ontological systems that have been derived from historically male dominated perspectives[89]. The character of Eleanor works as a feminist prototype, who achieved a critical and practical survey of the systems that beset her through strength of character and aristocratic positioning. Feminist critique of contemporary epistemological systems is successful to the extent that new 'feminist' knowledge is uncovered and made available for practical usage and everyday life. Ontological feminist critique is considered complex in that lifestyles derived from male dominated systems of thought are often thoroughly entrenched and difficult to dislodge[90]. For example, the knowledge systems of the royal family of Britain could include the record keeping, ledgers and historical accounts of the power structures that have maintained the royal family in their position through time. Open publication and close scrutiny of these knowledge sources reveals the ways in which the material flows of the royal family have transpired throughout history. Yet his new knowledge is not akin to changing the engrained habits, cultural formations and social rules of the royal family and their entourage. The ontology of the royal family is a complex and transversal system that takes elements of its historical heritage as the means to preserving and ritualising its continued existence. For example, the changing of the guards in London and the celebrations for the Queen's birthday across the world represent fixtures through which the royal family have reproduced and extended their existence through stylisation and form. The nature of this becoming and being has been abstracted and distanced from its sources until the re-enactment of these fixed points in the royal calendar transcend their physical and material bases. One could argue that the continued existence of the royal family becomes an endless succession of ritual and formalities meant to continue and extend their prestige yet also acting like an evacuation of life.

One can only speculate why Kate Middleton has fitted so neatly into the British royal system. From an immanent material perspective, the contrast with Lady Eleanor is striking. Eleanor mobilised forces across England and France to support her when she was queen and she kept elements of control over Aquitaine throughout her tempestuous relationship with Henry the II. Kate has quickly become cemented into the firmament of the royal legion and has seemingly let go of her previous existence to become a major ornament on the mantelpiece of the royal household. Perhaps Kate is so happy to have landed in the position as Duchess of Cambridge that she cannot raise her voice to question the ways in which this system is working. The analogy with a corporate employee is striking. Kate went through an elaborate and extended interview process from the time that she met Prince William to their marriage in 2011. After having passed all the aptitude tests during this period, she has been allowed into the family company on the proviso that she does not speak out or make any public statements regarding the running of the royal corporate machine. Eleanor had her own organisation that somewhat rivalled that of Henry, and was therefore free of this constraint and able to challenge the autocratic ways of her husband. Kate is a good corporate worker, whilst Eleanor was a CEO in her own right. One could say that Kate has not reignited the gender war that raged between Eleanor and Henry, and that erupted more recently between Diana and Charles, but has fitted in with the hegemony of Windsor Inc. Kate and Eleanor demonstrate very different subjective inclinations to being a royal, which are differentiated by historical context and relative positions of power. The immanence of Kate is imbricated within the combined influence of the royal family of Britain as media object, whilst Eleanor stands out as a royal historical character on her own, even having a mythological and romantic range of stories attached to her name with respect to the 'Court of Love' at Poitiers. Another aspect of the immanence of the plateau of 1150-1200 may be defined with respect to Deleuze and Guattari's concept of the war machine.

The war machine

The war machine is a central concept of *1000 Plateaus* and therefore vital to understanding the immanent materialism of this book. The thesis that Deleuze and Guattari put forward is connected to their conception of the nomad, and how this impinges upon consciousness, collectivity and life[91]. The nomad, as a form of habitation, subjectivity and desire needs nothing other than what is where he or she happens to be at any moment. For example, for hundreds of thousands of years, nomadic tribes of Homo sapiens followed herds of game animals across ancient plains before settling down in cities and establishing domesticated animal stock and agriculture. These ancient hunter/gatherer formations are continually played out, according to Deleuze and Guattari, in war. If one takes as an example, mediaeval Europe, where the feudal states were in danger from raids by plunderers from the East. The Mongols had evolved a sophisticated means of war involving horses and archers, who attacked and retreated quickly and in complex, changeable formations. This nomadic form of war often proved deadly against the slow, armoured European knights, who were either on foot or on horseback, and had lines of archers arranged in preset positions. The problematic for feudal European states to defend themselves against the incursions from the East and the Mongol hordes was set against the establishment of the Mongol Empire, the largest continuous land empire in history, which stretched across Asia from Mongolia to east Europe for one hundred and sixty years (1206-1368). However, as Deleuze and Guattari see it, the war machine always remains exterior to the state, therefore the ways in which the state must operate is to co-opt and entice the war machine to fight for it[92]. For example, Henry the II procured a war machine by hiring and paying mercenaries to act for him in the multiplicity of wars that he found himself embroiled within in the course of his term as lord and king in England and France.

The mercenary war machine and fledgling state system of Henry the II existed side-by-side, because the state of Henry was in its infancy and did not challenge the hegemony of the warriors who fought on its behalf. Problems arise when the war machine builds momentum and takes on pretentions to take over the state, as may occur during a coup d'état. The reality of the '1150-1200' plateau in Europe was that there were numerous war machines attached to local barons, kings and queens as well as roaming bands of mercenaries. Every territory in mediaeval Europe had a form of the state built around the ramparts of the castles, with tariffs, taxes, laws and pre-defined lord-serf relationships. The war machines of the knights and mercenary warriors fitted into these structures in terms of their defence and broke out of them in terms of fighting for their overlords or for the realm against exterior forces. One of the greatest causes for overt, exterior war of the period occurred in terms of the crusades at the decree of the Pope, where European warriors travelled to the Holy lands to liberate them from the Muslims. Henry the II imposed the 'Saladin Tithe' on his people to fund a crusade against the sultan Saladin, Lady Eleanor participated in the disastrous second crusade as queen of France with her husband at the time, King Louis VII. The crusades saw various developments in the war machines of knights, cavalry, archery, weapons, siege tactics, and land and sea travel, which were taken to another level by Henry and Eleanor's son, Richard the I (the Lionheart). Henry the II is renowned as being a state builder, who invented the system of the common law, and tried to make the barons and knights of the realm fully accountable to the Crown. In contrast, Richard the I is famous for his exploits as a warrior, and took part in and innovated with the war machine, especially in terms of its ability to function successfully on crusade. In terms of the plateau of '1150-1200' and its immanent materialism, the formation of war machines consisting of bands of knights working together for a cause, brings us to the infamous band of the 'Knights Templar' and their exploits in mediaeval Europe.

The Knights Templar (1119-1312) were an order of knights who came together to ostensibly protect pilgrimages to the Holy Lands. This function of the Knights Templar, which was at the bequest of the Pope, soon became elevated in Europe due to the power and influence of the Church and the importance assigned to the crusades. One could dispute the exact purpose of the twelfth- and thirteenth-century crusades, yet the role of the Knights Templar in their execution was pivotal. The knights became a wealthy, well-trained and lethal fighting brigade, which acted in the name of the Catholic Church, yet were ruthless and efficient in their tactics. The wealth of the brigade came from noblemen and pilgrims depositing their valuables with the Knights Templar before they went on pilgrimage. The Order in 1150 began generating letters of credit for pilgrims journeying to the Holy Land, pilgrims deposited their riches with a local Templar preceptory before embarking, received a document indicating the value of their deposit, they then used that document upon arrival in the Holy Land to recoup their funds. This new arrangement was a simple form of banking, and may have been the earliest formal system to use cheques; it improved the safety of pilgrims by making them less obvious targets for brigands, and it also contributed to the Templar purse. Based on this combination of donations and business dealing, the Templars made financial networks across the whole of Christendom. They bought large areas of land, both in Europe and the Middle East, they managed farms and vineyards, they built churches and castles, were involved in manufacturing, import and export businesses, they had their particular fleet of ships, and at one point they even owned the island of Cyprus. The Order of the Knights Templar potentially qualifies as the world's first multinational corporation as well as the proto-typical secret society.

In addition to their extraordinary financial and organisational skills, the Knights Templar were adept warriors, who combined the technical skill necessary to wield their weapons with the mental fortitude of absolute faith. According to Deleuze and Guattari the definition of a war machine includes a form of vitalism, which in the case of the Knight Templar, was a divine energy that went with them into battle and made them supposedly invincible to their enemies. The Knights Templar followed strict, monk-like lives, even though their Order became rich and powerful, they kept to absolute rules of behaviour and decorum or risked being ejected from the Order. The Order of the Knights Templar have become infamous as a proto-typical secret society, with their own codes and practices, and this is a form of organisation that became popular again in the nineteenth century and has been described in chapter 3 of this book. The power of the war machine works in this way, via intensity and selectivity, by encouraging a connection with nature through contemplation, and in having the flexibility to change one's approach given new contexts and conditions. The downfall of the Knights Templar came when King Philip IV of France, who was deeply in debt to the Knights, pressurized Pope Clement the V to disband the Order under the false charges of heresy and witchcraft. The leaders of the Order were burned at the stake and the official Catholic organisation of the Knights Templar was officially annulled in 1312, yet their legend and ideas have survived. The Knights Templar has an immanent and material presence today, due to the ways in which fighting forces absolutely committed to transcendent, religious values, still have impact and relevance, and the remnants of the mediaeval, holy conflict in the Middle East, especially in Israel.

One could argue that the jihadist, Muslim fighters of today, such as those associated with the El Qaeda movement, are the most similar to the Knights Templar. These fighters derive a type of holy energy from their quest to rid the world of the infidel non-Muslim through any means possible, especially self-sacrifice. The El Qaeda fighters and other associated groups have given rise to the continual state of the 'war on terror', which is the response of the bureaucratic and military state systems of the West to the threat of the war machines of the jihadists. In terms of the capitalised education of Kate Middleton, the most serious threat to her continued presence is probably a Qaeda-style terrorist attack, though she is mostly extremely well-guarded. In more general terms, attacks such as the recent decapitation of a British soldier close to his barracks in south London in May 2013, led to a wave of anti-Muslim and racist demonstrations in the UK, therefore strengthening the position of the state system and its 'war on terror'. Elite fighting forces within the military organ-isation of the West, such as the SAS in the UK or the Seals in the USA, emulate the notion of the war machine by encouraging small units of highly trained and well-motivated fighters. These units have autonomy in that their combat missions are most often classified secrets, such as the recent assassination of Osama Bin Laden in Pakistan. War machines emerge when seamless fighting brigades take on their own organisational character-istics, the collective ethos replacing the particular egos of individuals, the reasons and negotiations for war becoming secondary to the means of war feeding back into themselves as internal modes of production. War machines do nothing but make war, and are still relevant today in the dispersed, high tech battlefield, where killer drones are controlled thousands of kilometres from their targets in safe, military installations. The war machines carry on despite the application of high technology to the art of war, not because there is something uniquely human to making and maintaining war, but because there are singularities within the matrix of war making that cannot be replicated in sedentary or bourgeois life. In other words, the nomad breaks out at each interstices of war making, and defines a 'line of flight' away from and at odds with the various apparatuses of control of the state. However, to understand and express the material immanence of the '1150-1200' plateau further, one has to delve more profoundly into the remains of the mediaeval state system that has been left to us by Henry the II and his immediate successors, Richard and John.

Magna Carta

The writing of Magna Carta was completed and sealed by King John, 25 of his Barons, several other noblemen and their witnesses on June the 19th, 1215 in a meadow in Runnymede. The document, which means, 'Great Charter' was nearly a complete copy of an earlier document that had been formulated by Henry the I in 1100. The Barons of his realm, who wanted to secure certain rights and privileges under law, including the right to due process under the law of the land and not the arbitrary judgement of the king, had forced the Magna Carta on King John. In effect, Magna Carta adjusted and reconciled the common law of Henry the II with civil rights for freemen and the church, making the common law a system of interpersonal laws and not law by royal decree. The 1215 Magna Carta had 61 clauses, yet these were quickly reduced and several were changed as Magna Carta was reissued and republished with different clauses according to fluctuations in the political situation between the state and successive monarchies. The notion that we have of Magna Carta today is that it is one of the foundational documents that established freedoms under law, and this notion has been magnified in places such as the USA and Australia, where the common law of England was exported under British colonialism. For example, the constitution of the USA cites Magna Carta of Runnymede as a forerunner, in that certain freedoms such as the right to due process under the law of the land are recognised as applying to all men and women. In reality, Magna Carta was an agreement written under duress to secure the immediate future of King John by his rebellious barons. Several of its clauses were almost immediately renounced by King John, especially the infamous clause 61, which had given the barons the right to meet and claim assets of the monarch if the king had defied any of the clauses of Magna Carta. Furthermore, Magna Carta proved impossible to enforce against successive monarchs who openly manoeuvred to expand their power or vanquish their foes during the mediaeval period.

However, Magna Carta is an important mythological element of the state which we derive from the 1150-1200 plateau. Even though the state was shaped and designed by the monarchy, which is clear in the epoch of Henry the II and the common law, the assumption that we have today is that we have rights written into the running of the state and that it is not a system designed by the whims of the monarchy. In truth, Magna Carta was the first of a series of instruments that are now recognised as having a special constitutional status, the others being the Habeas Corpus Act (1679), the Petition of Right (1628), the Bill of Rights (1689), and the Act of Settlement (1701). The immanent materialism of the 1150-1200 plateau is constituted by the common law under Henry the II, and the state as a creation of the monarchy struggling with multiple factions in the realm including the Roman Catholic Church, the power of individual barons and Lady Eleanor of Aquitaine. The design and implementation of successive statute civil rights laws of parliament took place well after the reign of Henry the II, as the power of the monarchy was increasingly infringed upon by notions of rights that did not exist in the epoch of 1150-1200. In '1150-1200' civil rights only applied to noblemen or recognised members of the church, the rest of the population were serfs, who lived under the tutelage of the freemen, and had no freedoms as we might consider them today. Magna Carta is part of the immanent materialism of the plateau of 1150-1200 to the extent that we perceive rights and freedoms in the state that have supposedly been in place for hundreds of years. In reality, the power relationships between the monarch and the subjects of the realm are unequal under the law—the 'capitalised education' of Kate Middleton could be understood as a legal exception and not the norm, as she moves into the protective sphere of the monarchy.

Conclusion

Henry the II and Lady Eleanor are not ideal types that William and Kate have been imprinted upon, nor are they the romanticised heroes of a royal drama. Rather, the relationships between Henry and Eleanor and William and Kate, come together in a complex manner due to the philosophical backdrop of immanent materialism in this book. The most important aspect of these relationships is undoubtedly understood through the current monarch's continuing role as head of the state. Many of the factors and groupings of powers that have been analysed through this chapter are manifest in the role of the monarch with respect to the state, for example, in the questions regarding the legal framework of the common law and its application across the population. KM as media object will never be the head of the British state; however, she is now thoroughly involved with its machinations, as she has married the second in line of the British throne and she has given birth to the next king in line after that. Whilst KM as media object will not take on the political sovereignty of the monarch, as theorised, for example, by Hobbes, she does play a pivotal British role in the contemporary global environment of integrated world capitalism. In many ways therefore, KM as media object and a capitalised education have transcended the historical and power-related baggage that comes from the time of Henry the II and Lady Eleanor, 1150-1200. Yet this transcendence is also dependent on the material and immanent ways in which the period of 1150-1200 works to give power and affect to the present royal household, for example through the romantic stories of King Arthur and the Knights of Camelot. One could argue that the plateau of 1150-1200 plays a vital role in the set-up and delivery of the mythology of royalty, which still helps to power KM as media object and a capitalised education.

Chapter 7

Future(s) capital and lifelong learning:

Kate Middleton (KM)
April 29th, 2011

Introduction

This chapter describes the last plateau in the series of this book that combine to make up the influence of Kate Middleton (KM) on contemporary life. The intensities that pass along the surface of this plateau are therefore the most familiar to us, as they happened only recently, yet the very familiarity of this passing can make the description and analysis of this plateau confusing and strange. In contrast to, for example, chapter 6, and the plateau of 1150-1200, that is anchored in historical and documented events and their relevance to today, the discernment of what counts as an immanent material effect of April the 29th, 2011, is harder to definitely ascertain or localise. In part, this is an important aspect of immanent materialism as a method and a means to understand what is happening to us in terms of how we relate to KM. Clearly, if one lives in a part of the world without television, where English isn't spoken, or where the British colonialists never ventured, the influence of KM on one's subjectivity might be very slim. In contrast, if one has grown up in an English speaking country with a connection to the UK and the world's media, KM appears like an organising principle of our lives, her every breath and move being scrutinised and endlessly photographed. How can we make sense of that? What are the political, social and cultural ramifications of introducing Kate to the world's public and making her the centre of the current media circus? As you read these words, Kate & William's first child George has been born and the media's spotlight has been shifted somewhat from Kate to the new baby. Yet one could argue that certain driving principles remain in place even if Kate loses her pre-eminence as the image, face and body of the royal family, for example, that there is an immutable connection between the media and the royals, and that their privilege and place in the world and the constituents of a system in which they exist is unassailable. The purpose of applying immanent materialism to the focus of KM and the plateau of April the 29th, 2011, is precisely to open up and craft a means to looking and under-standing beyond the conditions of the current situation, which are described in this book as a capitalised education. Why isn't the media directed more towards the non-royals? What are the implications of not being trapped by the matrix of finance, image and celebrity that propels KM into a place in our lives?

The immanent materialism of this chapter opens up these questions and there are, of course, others that will be examined with respect to the plateau of April the 29th, 2011. One has to go beyond the subjectivity of the moment and the romanticism of the royal wedding to understand the multiple driving factors at work as the gathered congregation listened to the solemn words of the current Archbishop of Canterbury. The essential thesis of this chapter and in turn of the whole book is that there is a connection between the state of contemporary society, which is characterised by global post-industrial capitalism, and the subjectivity of being part of the worldwide audience for the events of April the 29th, 2011. One of the major problems with this thesis is the mutative, adaptable and multi-pronged nature of contemporary capitalism. Commentators have spoken about affective and cognitive capitalism, finance capitalism, immaterial and digital labour[93]. How can one make sense of the profusion of explicative frames that beset one when trying to understand how contemporary society works? Certainly, the landscapes of factories, owners, workers, property and investment capital that Marx described in the nineteenth century has become infinitely more saturated and inter-related, even though the divisions between the rich and the poor have not been eliminated, as many experiments in communal society have been left behind or swallowed up by and in mainstream, capitalist life. This chapter will tread an immanent and material line between the character-istics of contemporary society in order to explicate the evolution of KM as media object and as an intimate subject in our thinking and learning minds of everyday life (a capitalised education).

The thought of lifelong learning

Martin Heidegger philosophised about the place of thinking in terms of being, difference and the extrapolation from the repetition of the same. For Heidegger, the philosophical act is one of understanding origins and beginnings, of investigating being, of unearthing what is primal and complicit in the thought from within, and ultimately, the act is about the destruction of western metaphysics which he saw as the history of the forgetting of being. Heidegger's philosophical investigations led him back to the Greek origins of Western thought and to explaining how concepts and ideas arose in that cauldron of thought, creativity and development[94]. In contrast, Deleuze examines thought in terms of a violence, as a harsh interruption in the continuity of things, and in the ways in which being has broken out and revolutionised the self. Deleuze considers the origins of Western thought in Greek philosophy as being an accident, as defining an abhorrent other caused by immigration, the Greeks learnt to think otherwise through contact with the outside world and as an internal disruption to their systems and established ways of doing things, in other words, philosophy is an anathema. In sum, Heidegger thought difference as continuity, whereas Deleuze thinks the difference of difference, which he termed as the 'differ-enciator'[95]. Today, we are beset by learning theory that one could argue imposes systems on thought in terms of lifelong learning and continual adaptation, and lifelong learning is connected to the precarity of work, and with the limited or deficit outlook of having one set of unchangeable knowledge skills for life[96]. One may define the debate on lifelong learning in terms of Heidegger and Deleuze's approach to thought, Heidegger emphasising a benign understanding of lifelong learning in terms of the concept helping us to adapt and survive in times of economic and financial crisis, whilst Deleuze emphasises the violence and imposition of lifelong learning, as being an aggressive invasion and a set of restrictions and limitations on the creativity and originality of thought.

Deleuze's objection to lifelong learning is that it predisposes learning in terms of an entrapped outlook on life. One could ask about non-learning, un-learning or moments when one is just floating along or playing? Deleuze argues for a form of 'drifting' in terms of learning, where one discovers pre-personal singularities, and they stick to the body as knowledge and as a function of memory. At these moments, one is torn apart, as one learns something new and original knowledge fields are opened up that were hitherto unimaginable[97]. Deleuze is importantly pointing to a restructuring of the unconscious that occurs when one learns, and he notes how the unconscious restructuring ripples through one's consciousness as the realisation of something new or novel and in terms of what he calls, after Bergson, 'the virtual'. Deleuze's view on learning is importantly not dualistic, but sets up a continuum of differentials wherein learning can happen through a new system of philosophy which redraws Kant's notions of the faculties to make learning, un-learning and non-learning part of the multiplicities that one has at one's disposal to think immanently. Thinking for Deleuze is therefore not necessarily critical, as in the *Critique of Pure Reason*, but the power of criticality is not excluded or diminished from thought by applying Deleuze's system. Deleuze's system augments the power of thought by redrawing the potential dualisms between thought and unthought or learning and non-learning. Instead, we have a means to bring together the rational and irrational objects of the mind under what he terms in *Difference and Repetition*, and with reference to Kant, as transcendental empiricism, and which is translated into immanent materialism in *1000 Plateaus* which he wrote with Félix Guattari. Deleuze extends and rebranches Heidegger's formula for thought by delving into the unconscious and by adding to the ways in which Heidegger conceives of and uses the power of philosophy. Deleuze adds non-philosophical and un-philosophical thought as streamed responses to phenomena and empirical objects that pass through consciousness such as KM as media object in this book. The point of the analysis here is that Deleuze's approach helps us to undo the connection between time and learning that one may find in lifelong learning.

What is the time of lifelong learning? One could argue that the time of lifelong learning is akin to eternity, to an endless, ubiquitous moment when one learns at every age and in any context, formal or non-formal. On one hand, the extension of learning and the investigation and characterisation of learning from formal situations in schools, institutes and universities, to everyday and de-institutionalised contexts, makes the likelihood of recognising and understanding the multiple and subtle ways in which one learns greater. On the other hand, the very ubiquity of the time of learning in lifelong learning makes it more likely that trivial and non-assessable forms of learning are included in what we term as learning. In contrast to a set exam on literacy or numeracy skills, which will have definite results that can be fed into understanding the literacy or numeracy skills of the agent, the results of lifelong learning are clearly not assessable in such a clear-cut and quantitative manner. What does it mean to say that we learn all the time and in every context? How can the notion of lifelong learning help us to develop useful knowledge skills if it involves sometimes trivial and non-assessable matters? I would like to suggest that the answers to these two questions come in the undoing of the connections between lifelong learning and time, as if lifelong learning was a form of prison sentence or entrapment. There is clearly a very positive side to recognising the subtle and practical ways in which one may learn in de-institutionalised contexts, but at the same time, one does not always learn in these contexts. One has to recognise that non-formal contexts have a landscape and set of priorities written into them, that there are singularities, to use Deleuze's phrase that he borrowed from Gilbert Simondon[98], in terms of aspects of becoming and intensification that can join together and form the strange attractors in life that go on to define our characters and show us how conditioning works. In this book, the principal strange attractor is Kate Middleton, here defined as KM, media object and with a resulting capitalised education in which we partake.

The relevant question for this book and chapter is: Why and how does KM as media object become imprinted in our minds as a learning object? The why of the question refers to and uncovers the assemblages behind the presentation of KM as media object. These groupings may be commercial or royal and are inculcated in the social and cultural processes around KM. Commercial interests want us to learn about KM to sell new ranges of clothes, or to buy into any products connected to the royal family. The royal interests at work in KM as media object are interested in the presentation of a modern celebrity front for the royal family that hides the inequity of the situation and disguises the historical and power-based fault lines that have propelled the royal family of Britain into their current state of pre-eminence and capitalisation in the world system. KM as media object in royal terms is a recent corporate recruit who can simultaneously sell a normative and continuing message about the royals through her image, and strengthen the blood-line. The how aspect of the question around KM as media and learning object is a reflexive one connected to the current state of the media and the means deployed by media producers to bridge the gaps between media content and subjectivity. One could frame this aspect of lifelong learning and KM as media object as a war of semiotics, designed to entrap and seduce one's thinking habits[99]. The current devolution of the media from prestigious national carriers of the news, to the micro-provision on every mobile phone on the planet as a potential media device connected to the internet, has resulted in new tactics and new pathways from 'the news' to the mind. KM as media object fits into these pathways because her appealing image has been utterly stripped of meaning or connection with the political and historical baggage that surrounds the royal family. KM as media object sits happily and unquestioningly on our micro mobile media devices, as there is no room in this context for political or social analysis of the economy that surrounds KM.

In contrast, this book has provided an immanent material analysis of the situation, framed around plateaus, and doing work in terms of showing how the political and social economies of KM have been built up through time. The plateaux add a non-linear element to the historical build-up of power and influence of the royal family of Britain, which parallels the ways in which capitalism has come to dominate all other systems of social and cultural production. KM as media object fits into the present manifestation of global capitalist life because her image and character are expressions of a corporate and social-climbing reorganisation of the drives. This reorganisation in the ways in which one is motivated to live has been reproduced and copied around the globe, as particular communities move from subsistence and local contexts to be connected to a global community that imbibes and aspires to internationalisation. However, this internationalisation is not an egalitarian redistribution of identity between equal partners in different parts of the world. There is a global imbalance in power that is reflected in the media and capitalism, and KM as media object is a definite sign and part of this imbalance. For example, villagers in Indonesia, hooked up to the internet, or receiving satellite television news, are bombarded by stereotypes and images from Western corporate and celebrity culture. KM as media object fits in with these stereotypes and images, and may be consumed by the Indonesian villagers as a normative aspect of what it means to conform to globalised values today. Such an 'exchange' lacks any analysis or understanding of the political or social consequences of KM as media object. The villagers receive KM as media object as part of their everyday life and learn about her as if she is reflecting their very desire to be happy and rich. KM is henceforth incorporated into the collective unconscious of the village, and her appearance in any form is latterly a marker or differenciator in Deleuze's terms of what makes life meaningful or good. As a result, young girls copy KM's style without realising or recognising the fact, young men desire KM as an aspirational partner, even though she is really only a media object, projected into their homes by commercial and royalist interests unimaginable from their dislocated and remote perspective. Part of this disconnection between media reality and localised realities designates and requires an understanding of the dynamics involved with the current state of capitalism.

Future(s) capital and speculation

Contemporary commentators such as Maurizio Lazzarato and Christian Marazzi have noted the general dynamics of the current stage of global capitalism as being attuned to financialisation[100]. This means that finance capitalism has taken over and replaced other forms of capitalism based on manufacturing or agriculture, and finance is now the dominant organising factor in terms of what makes the world system of capital exchange function. This fundamental change in the way that capitalism works has not happened overnight, but has taken root through world trade centres in London, New York and Hong Kong, that have increasingly linked individual markets through cybernetic and electronic means. The planet Earth now has a world system of international finance that moves in every direction and across cybernetic networks, and is controlled by computers and traders who monitor and speculate on every product, company share price or bond through algorithms and charts that examine any fluctuation in price or variable factor that could possibly determine or change that price in the future. The recent Global Financial Crisis (GFC) in 2008 opened up and stopped this complex inter-related system for a moment, as the machinations of the world of finance was suddenly exposed by the failure of the subprime mortgage market in the USA. On one level, one can easily understand that the lending practice to households who could not pay back the aggregate from spiralling interest rate hikes on their mortgages was unsustainable, yet what was uncovered by the GFC were the complex and inter-related derivative and finance packages that bundled these toxic loans along with multiple other deals. The toxicity of the subprime loans was hidden, disguised and passed on, so that banks and public taxpayer systems around the globe ended up with unpayable debts that they simply had to write off. One could argue that such enormous injustice and unaccountability is a contemporary fact and basis for the current system of financial capitalism[101].

Financial capitalism is neither moral nor responsible for its actions, other than with respect to making a profit. Rather, capital flows around the globe are specifically designed to escape the attention of individual state governments and the wishes of populations, through loopholes in tax law or by pressurising legislators to deregulate their markets in the name of freedom and through free trade agreements. Such processes have produced a narrative that we are now living through, and that is immanent in terms of the plateau of April the 29th, 2011, which depends on the *a priori* capitalised position. The recent story of the royal family of Britain is one of capitalisation in terms of their holdings, properties, brand name, their regular tax payer funded income and various inter-related royal companies and fund interests, including charities. For example, the royal family indirectly own many of the seabeds around the UK through the Crown Estate. These seabeds are now the sites for wind farms, which have increased considerably in value due to the current state of global climate change—a.k.a. climate collapse— and with the connected green economy becoming exponentially more lucrative. Furthermore, the Crown Estate, that is a public company connected to the royal family, owns a lot of the property in Regent Street in London and elsewhere, which has become more valuable as the financialisation of world capitalism has dramatically increased the divisions between the rich and the poor. Regent Street is now a consumer playground for the mega-rich and the aspiring rich, who inhabit the designer stores in order to use their surplus capital and to buy luxury items. Finance capitalism takes the facts of the increasing importance of capitalisation, market domination by a very few mega-rich, and the disparities between the rich and the poor as given, as traders and computer programmed algorithms calculate the flux in the markets, and analyse the trends within any fixed points of price in order to make tendential profits. For example, shares in royal companies look increasingly attractive due to the strength of the established capitalisation position through their violent history, green companies attract venture and risk capital, because the profit margins are potentially extraordinary. As a consequence, share trading practises work off systems that involve making profits from the aspirations of non-capitalised populations, and which constitute emergent markets, and from environmental disasters and their technological solutions. At the same time as market trading practices explore communities of the poor and environmental ruin for profit, flows of tax payer money have increasingly become a target for capital interest, in terms of blended and mixed sources of income and stripping publically held assets to increase bulk capital potential.

In terms of education, finance capitalism is only interested in private ventures, charter schools, and looking at ways in which public, tax payer funded assets may be sold off or blended with private money to make a profit. Stephen Ball has charted many of these forces and battlegrounds in his recent books about the current world system of capitalism and education[102]. In terms of our focus on KM as media object, the Middleton family used their capital from their online business, 'Party Pieces', and possibly some inheritance money, to fund Kate through one of England's most prestigious private schools, Marlborough College, and later to attend and study at St. Andrew's College in Scotland, where she met Prince William. The Middleton family put their capital to work through the progress and transformation of Kate from an upwardly mobile middle class young woman, to wife of the second heir to the throne of England. This investment in their daughter by the Middleton family has paid off, because Kate has now joined the royal household as the Duchess of Cambridge and has produced a son for the royal lineage to carry on into the future. Importantly, the influence of the capital at the disposal of the royal family and the celebrity of Kate as KM, media object, has influenced and aggregated the capital flows of the Middleton family. Their online business, which depends on internet hits and interest generated in their products, has, by association with the royal family and the popularity of Kate, become much more lucrative. Such a result and increase in fortunes for the Middleton family shows us in part how finance capitalism works with respect to and in relation with the electronic networks and media outlets that functions in tandem with the assemblages of finance capitalism.

Finance capitalism has no respect for or interest in communities, unless there is a profit to be made by exploiting some aspect of their needs or by taking over community interests in terms of capitalised positions. In the case of the Middleton family and their early venture into electronic business in the late 1980s, finance capitalists would have been reluctant to back a business that has a low profit base in terms of product pricing and is faced with fierce international competition. Finance capitalists would have asked these questions to the Middleton family: Who wants to buy the products that 'Party Pieces' has for sale, i.e. what is the market? How can profit be made from their online business operations, and how can these operations be made more efficient? What is the sustainability of their business model into the future? After and through the plateau of April the 29th, 2011, these questions have become irrelevant. The 'Party Pieces' brand name has become valuable in itself, because of Kate's fame, and due to her connection with and participation in a fully capitalised, royal position. The consequence for the online business model of 'Party Pieces' is that their web site now receives heavy traffic due to curious surfers who may have heard about the business through media reports regarding Kate and the ubiquitous coverage that KM as media object now receives. 'Party Pieces' has not suddenly become a different or better company, but currently basks in the limelight of their most famous daughter and her involvement with historical wealth. The Middleton family have gone from the pre 'Party Pieces' salaried existences working in the airlines, to online e-entrepreneurs, to *de facto* members of the British aristocracy through the marriage of their daughter to William. Finance capitalism is not interested in the social or cultural aspects of Kate Middleton's story, but understands that there are profits to be made from her media exposure and any connection with such a wholly capitalised position as that of the royal Windsor family. These aspects of finance capitalism bring to the fore the connection between lifelong long learning and future(s) capital, which is 'time' and which anchors the immanence of the plateau of the 29th of April 2011. Lifelong learning induces a questioning and understanding of intimate and objective time in terms of what and how one learns, future(s) capital involves being able to speculate on the flux of the present in terms of the profit-based possibilities of the future. Coincidentally, these questions about time fundamentally concern a great deal of contemporary continental philosophy.

Time and thought

Contemporary continental philosophy sits in the pivot of a crossroads between the legacy of 1970s left wing political theorising and the nineteenth-century concern for science. One could perhaps characterise such a crossroads through the work of François Laruelle, and his non-philosophy. Laruelle places concentrated meaning and importance in scientific statements that have predictive power in the world, such as Einstein's equation of relativity, $E=mc^2$, yet Laruelle simultaneously wants to evolve a system of philosophical thought that effectively deals with the current state of world capitalism and its effects such a nihilism. Laruelle's solution to the requirements of a politics that has scientific validity is to turn to non-philosophy, which is a non-standard approach to thinking, and which advances a form of scepticism with respect to matter and ideals, for example:

> To talk of matter, to designate either it or the sciences of matter, isn't sufficient in order to produce a genuinely materialist assertion, or even—which would only be one of its traits among others—an immanent one. The problem here is no longer that of a 'materialist' discourse or knowledge of matter, but of an utterance that would itself be intrinsically material— which, as anyone will admit, isn't bound to turn that utterance into a thing just because one would no longer make of it a discourse about a thing.[103]

Laruelle is searching for a mode of speaking and thinking that circumvents the assumptions of both normative materialism and idealism. Non-philosophy contends that other modes of thought are possible that allow for and encourage political statements about the world which match with material realities, i.e. do not contain ideological or hidden agendas. I would suggest that such an aim is aligned with the immanent materialism derived from Deleuze and Guattari in this book, which is a form of materialism that is both politically motivated and describes the processes of empirical reality in the world[104]. Non-philosophy and immanent materialism are not identical, but do share commonalities and purposes in the similar uptake of science and politics. One parallel concern for non-philosophy and immanent materialism is the importance of time and the insertion of 'space-time' since Einstein into the way that one thinks and acts in the world. Einstein's insights into matter, energy and time have revolutionised Newton's mechanical picture of a clockwork universe and has helped to produce the field of quantum mechanics, which attempts to describe the ways in which bodies and objects relate to one another relatively. The dimension of space-time is fundamental to quantum mechanics because it unhinged the Newtonian conception of space and time as being set on two separate axes. One could argue that Einstein's deterministic understanding of space-time as the fourth dimension does limit its applicability here as a philosophical concept, or of being capable to enable the thought of time necessary to link lifelong learning and future(s) capital[105]. However, Einstein does give us the necessary platform of thought to unhinge the notion that time flows through us in a regular manner and without impacting on matter, by creating its own complex dimension wherein relativity is possible.

The important analytical praxis for us to understand for this chapter is the way in which time may be thought for the plateau of April the 29th, 2011. In one way, time was slowed down and molecularised by the royal wedding, the timeless royal ceremony and elaborate costumes and arrangements adding to the perception of infinite time dimensionality of the event, in terms of making one believe that the wedding had always happened and was a repetition of an infinite number of royal occasions in the past. Yet simultaneous and complementary to the slowing down and stretching out of time due the elaborate staging and references to other royal occasions, was the means to broadcast the wedding globally, to store the footage and to analyse what was happening in real time, i.e. accelerating the end of the wedding event, as just another block of global media time. Therefore, one could argue that time was slowed down and accelerated through and via the plateau of April the 29th, 2011, creating turbulence and a maelstrom of time. Within this maelstrom, and on the political level, the royal wedding was a complete show of power, and a reaffirmation of the stability and durability of the royal family as the premier social-cultural grouping in the UK and across the world. Such a politics of the royal wedding could lead to negativity, cynicism and a dispiriting in revolutionary politics that looks to theorise change in and through the plateau of April the 29th, 2011. For example, there were media reports on the day of the royal wedding of the enormous police operation that was mounted on April the 29th, 2011 in central London to make sure that no protest groups or anarchists were able to approach or make their voices heard anywhere near the events of the royal wedding. One can see from these facts how the British state works in unison with the royal family to control any dissent or interruption to the unfolding of the presentation of continuous royal power. As a homogenised audience, we are meant to wave flags, cheer, wish the royal couple all the best, and perhaps comment on the elegance of KM, who was the centrepiece of the orchestrated pageantry.

Finance capitalism sits in an accelerated dimension of time-space where deals are able to be completed instantaneously across the globe. Yet this accelerated dimension is able to recognise and adjust to the historical repetitions of events such as the royal wedding with its impression of timelessness, because the representation of power is extremely attractive to financial flows in terms of capitalisation. The royal family displayed their social and cultural capital in and through the plateau of April the 29th, 2011, as well as the inter-related effects, such as the control of the state through the mounting of the police guard around the royal festivities. Market traders can be reassured by April the 29th, 2011 that the UK is not moving towards a republic, so shares and interest in the stocks of the royals look increasingly attractive, as well as investment in their inter-related businesses and any services that are connected to the royal family. Furthermore, the celebrity status of Kate Middleton has been confirmed by the plateau of April the 29th, 2011. Increased interest and a maelstrom of relativity around KM as media object has been created, and, one could add, her own space-time dimension, in which she now acts, and where the abstract forces of trade and power collide and compete for attention. KM's dimension of space-time has come about because Kate is, in effect, separate from the royal cohort. She is not saddled by the power-related scandals of the past that have cast a shadow over many of the royal family and its functioning as an ensemble. For example, when it was revealed that Charles had been having an affair with Camilla Parker-Bowles whilst still married to Diana, his popularity plummeted in contrast to the 'People's Princess'. KM as media object comes from outside of these internal conflicts, which probably would have been buried and forgotten in the past, she comes as an outsider who can make a difference to the fortunes of Windsor plc.

Kate Middleton has helped to rescue and promote the popularity of the British royal family. She comes across as a sensible, well-mannered young woman, now a mother, but also a hard-working member of the royal cohort. Any comments from any quarter that are critical of Kate Middleton at all are roundly rebuffed by David Cameron and others with expressions such as,

"Kate is good for Britain". What he really means when he says these words is that the space-time dimension in which KM as media object now sits, works through global finance capitalism to incur capital growth. I doubt whether David Cameron or other members of parliament would defend the rest of the royal family in this way, except perhaps William or the Queen. KM's image and demeanour make unrivalled perturbations in the world's media circus, she is the humble girl who has come good, she presents a quiet, good-looking aspect to being aspirational and conservative, and wanting to join the world's elite without having to work around the clock or just being exceptionally lucky, and with the most probably result of failure. Kate represents a calm and gentle approach to success. Yet underneath this outward demeanour and image, there lies her story and background that have pushed her to be in the contemporary position as KM, media object, and on the plateau of April the 29th, 2011 as the central player.

The doppelgänger-effect

The previous plateau to this chapter and the royal wedding of April the 29th, 2011, was that of 31st of August, 1997 (see chapter 1) and concerned the death of Diana Spencer. In non-linear terms, all plateaux in this book can work on and construct the effects of KM as media object and a capitalised education in complex and inter-related ways, yet as a precedence and incidence of learning, what happened to Diana in and through the plateau of August the 31st, 1997 is of paramount importance to KM as media object and the assemblages that have brought her to such a point in the world. Diana was well-loved by the general public and had been a media sensation, yet had fallen out of favour with the royal family after separating from Charles, and had explained the revelations about their private life together in a media interview. At the time of her death, Diana had been ostracised from royal circles and had been leading a new life with Dodi Al-Fayed, the son of the Egyptian tycoon and then owner of Harrods, Mohamed Al-Fayed. The two princes, William and Harry were sheltered from the storm that surrounded the death of Diana by the royal family and their father, Charles, yet the effects of their mother's sudden departure must have been devastating. By all accounts, Diana had been a warm and loving mother, and even though she had been separated from their father for several years before her death, the shock of her sudden loss would have been enormous. Three years later, William went to college at St. Andrew's, where he met Catherine Middleton, who would become his wife in 2011. Catherine Middleton is named as such at this time, because she had to use her elite education at Marlborough College in order to fit in with the social scene at St. Andrew's and to move in the same circles as Prince William, and she had not yet become Kate (KM), the media object.

To surmise that Catherine replaced Diana in William's life at this early stage would be an overstatement. Rather, Catherine became a confidant and aide to William in a troubled time away from the royal fold and when he was trying to find his own way in the world and cope with his mother's death. William seems to be an inward and quietly spoken individual, who would have been deeply hurt by the death of his mother in his teenage years. However, the immanent material analysis of this book does not include conspiracy theories about the evolution of KM into the royal fold or the death of Diana, nor does it propose psychologising accounts of the ways in which William and Catherine came together. Rather, the material facts of what happened are joined through immanence to the development of KM as media object via her passage through Marlborough, St. Andrew's and beyond. The full-blown capitalised education of KM as media object comes about through the entire plane of the plateau of April the 29th, 2011, and its complete interconnected matrix (chapters 1-6). The doppelgänger-effect is a part of this matrix and an important aspect of its development, one that is enhanced by the media and through learning. The doppelgänger-effect starts to emerge later in the relationship between the young couple, once Catherine had established contact with William, but before their relationship had been formalised.

In the ten years between Catherine and William meeting at St. Andrew's and their royal wedding, Catherine frequently dressed in the same clothes as Diana Spencer at royal social events. During this time, her public image was reengineered and began to emerge as a new whole—Catherine becomes Kate, beloved to the people, and the replacement to the 'People's Princess', Diana Spencer, who had died so dramatically in 1997. Kate replaces Diana in the public's mind and in their clamour for a sympathetic royal personage, untouched by scandal or locked in the prison of manners, distance and coldness that ties up the royal subjects in their subjective privileged cages, unable to relate to the 'common man'. Kate was positioned to replace Diana in the hearts of the public and Prince William, even though he could freely choose any woman that he wanted. Kate appeared and reappeared in his life during this period; she was the ghost of his mother, the most photographed woman in the world, until she transforms into KM, media object, and the new target of the paparazzi. The media need a story and Kate's rise to fame and on-off affair with the prince is superb material for any photo-shoot or gossip column. Only the prince understands his true affections, yet his ultimate liaison and marriage to Kate, who comes from a different world to his closed royal life, must have seemed like a destiny, as she mimicked the dead Diana. William finds Kate and rediscovers Diana, his mother, and this closes the oedipal circle. Such forces at work in the life of William are invisible, yet such invisibility is the necessary condition for the doppelgänger-effect to work. Invisibility is not a neutral or passive state, but a precise disguise that works to substitute one subject for another. Kate is a doppelgänger, able to mimic and replace the dead subject through gesture, voice, dress and presence, and the readily available public record of Diana's life which was photographed and written about *ad nauseam*. Kate was placed into the memory folds of Diana. One must realise that these collective memory folds are affective because the paparazzi killed Diana, and they can revive her memory by capturing Kate on film. These social, media based and economic procedures have vital energies, directions, and are positioned in space-time as has been argued above. Diana as media object had her own entourage and back story, KM has taken over and replaced many of these factors that push the media, learning, power and economics together (a capitalised education). KM is now the most photographed woman in the world, and her ability to take over Diana's role as public figure has seen her popularity rise to an extraordinary zenith. Yet where does the doppelgänger-effect leave us in terms of immanent materialism and the politics of this plateau?

Occupy everything

KM as media object works through doubling and as a double to the time-space that was created by the plateau of Diana Spencer, and as a destiny and result of every plateaux in this book—a capitalised education. Yet the political landscape that KM as media object creates has many other factors, assemblages and forces running through it. For example, the ways in which corporate culture and its mores have crossed over and proliferated in everyday life, make the politics of KM as media object dependent upon and related to the ways in which corporate life now permeates everything that we do. One could argue that the politics of the takeover of everyday life by corporate culture goes back to the 1980s, where neoliberal regimes in the UK and the USA drove market-forces and private interests into every public concern (see chapter 1). Union power and left-wing politics were dissolved under pressure from Margaret Thatcher, Ronald Reagan and their respective governments. Every successive government in the neoliberal democracies of the West have had to readjust and realign themselves with respect to the economic rationality of the 1980s, which had produced the present climate where market forces are tasked to solve social problems in areas, for example, such as education, which is one of the dual concerns of this book. KM as media object fits in with such a political atmosphere because of the commercial and capitalised forces that flow through KM's time-space. One cannot associate any left-wing or communitarian political stance with KM as media object, even though she has been intermittently engaged with charity work in her role as the Duchess of Cambridge. Rather, the machine of global financial capitalism sits comfortably with her position as the new corporate employee and PR face of Windsor plc.

The most prevalent and ubiquitous political movement since the 2008 GFC, and which coincides with the politics of the plateau of April the 29th, 2011, is the 'occupy movement'. With mainstream right and the left wing political parties offering similar neoliberal solutions to social problems, and, even worse, being simultaneously manipulated behind the scenes by the forces of global financial capitalism, the occupy movement suggests a withdrawal from the very notion of representation in political terms. Marco Deseriis and Jodi Dean name the occupy movement as 'the movement without demands' in contradiction to mainstream political manoeuvring, or to the protest movements of the past, which set out clear agendas and strategies to address their demands[106]. In contrast, the occupy movement works in the gaps of linguistic signification and has no specific or directed statements that designate their political stance on issues such as the GFC or the contemporary indebt-edness of student-life. Rather, the occupy movement does not pretend to have instrumental solutions to social problems, but advocates the occupation of the sites of crisis, such as Wall Street, or the meetings of the G20, and other political-economic macro organisational locations. Deseriis and Dean argue that the occupy movement is unsustainable precisely due to the lack of demands and strategies to achieve any goals, in contrast, for example, to revolutionary communism that posits the overthrow of existing imperial-capitalist structures and their support networks, or ecological movements that seek to address the imbalances in the environment. Deseriis and Dean argue that the autonomist and anti-representational core of the occupy movement fails to deal with the real issues of inequality and power that exist in capitalism such as the domination of private investment and capitalisation in, for example, the property market.

However, I would like to counter that the anti-representational and autonomist core of the occupy movement is precisely its strength. One can easily become exhausted by protesting against everything that is inequitable within the current capitalism world system, without gain and without success. Rather, these very energies of complaint may be co-opted and used by capitalists to make a profit, as any identifiable group can be rationalised into a consumer market with a definite subjectivity and henceforth sold products according to their desires. One could argue that the anti-representation and autonomy of the occupy movement is a deliberate and sophisticated political strategy designed to obscure the identities of the subjects who occupy, and the collective mentality of the occupy movement. Trying to completely step outside of capitalist control and organisation of thought is increasingly impossible, as the ways in which profit is determined comes from many regions, from the concrete reality of property ownership to the immaterial digital labour of Facebook. The occupy movement moves between these fixtures of profit and control smoothly, and creates a different place amidst the structures of current capitalist functioning. For example, in Wall Street, the occupation created a carnival atmosphere amongst the usually bleak ramparts of the inner city New York financial district. Intellectuals spoke to the crowd through repetition of their words, because microphones and the amplification of voices were banned, musicians turned up and played for free. A news-worthy media event was created that highlighted the profit margins and criminality of the big companies, whilst the majority paid for the financial mistakes that belied the GFC through taxation and austerity. For a moment, something new happened in this place of endless profit-seeking and digital deals, until the inevitable repression by the state acting to preserve the normative running of financial capitalism. The police moved in with their dogs and batons to clear the New York occupy crowd and their tents, however, the idea and politics of 'occupy everything' lives on, and can be resynthesised for our purposes in the analysis of the plateau of April the 29th, 2011 and KM as media object.

The political frontage of KM as media object is complex and riddled with multiple power concerns—commercial, corporate, conservative and royalist—as has been noted above. One cannot direct occupy KM as media object, yet the political strategies of anti-representation and autonomy do give one a framework whereby the influence of KM as media object on subjectivity may be addressed. This influence may be summed up through the phrase, 'semiocapitalism' or semiotic capitalism, which is derived from the research of Félix Guattari[107]. Guattari realised in the 1970s that capitalism now works through a regime of signs that impinge upon and condition subjectivity. The most prescient form of semiocapitalism is advertising, which bombards consciousness with consumer messages, and looks at any strategy, both conscious and unconscious, to enter into one's thoughts. Inside of the bombardment of advertising is the core notion of capital, and differentiated flows of capital, which advertising ties to an extraordinary array of benefits, such as health, good looks, attractiveness and success. The processes of semiocapitalism hollow out and transform subjectivity, until the desire for capital replaces any other desire and becomes the subject's primary motivation and reason to live. Guattari explored these effects through his theoretical writing, experimental anti-psychiatric group sessions and creative therapies, and came up with the means to resist the take-over of subjectivity by capital, both in an intellectual and practical sense[108]. KM as media object is a contemporary example of how such a take-over can happen, because KM as media object produces an irresistible relationship with capital, both in terms of Kate's capitalised education and the broad social and cultural assemblages that line up behind and through Kate's actions.

One cannot directly oppose KM as media object, even though one may ignore the signs connected to KM, so to speak. News of the recent birth of Kate and William's son, George Alexander Louis, filled up the daily newspapers in the UK to any extraordinary extent. One might say that this profusion of signs connected to KM as media object could be side stepped or ignored simply by not reading the newspapers, yet such a conscious avoidance does nothing to diminish the powerful interconnectivity and matrix of KM as media object. The anti-representative, autonomous option that is exemplified by the occupy movement, does not pretend that KM as media object is neutral, irrelevant or impotent, but finds creative and new ways to analyse and enunciate the influence of KM as media object. Guattari's methods of analysis and enunciation were known as 'transversalism' and 'cartography', and they are collective, experimental and pragmatic ways of making groups work in unison through, for example: writing poetry, singing songs, doing philosophy, making art, using media such as the radio to transmit revolutionary messages, and in today's environment, finding creative and new means to deploy electronic communications, whether they are in the form of blogs, Facebook or on YouTube. In the context of KM as media object, the experimental practises would be connected to exploring and unhinging the ways in which Kate can be become fixated in consciousness, due to the extraordinary media coverage which her image and personality currently enjoys.

Even though the occupy movement cannot literally occupy KM as media object, they could occupy areas connected to the royal family of Britain, or at least until they are moved on by the police! Whilst the occupy movement occupies areas connected to the royal family, they will produce a festival atmosphere which critically and creatively examines the role of KM as media object in contemporary society and on subjectivity. This critical and interactive examination could be in the form of KM poetry, painting or installation art, drama, music or philosophy. The point is not to form one fixed or static view of KM as media object, but to reflect the complex and inter-related ways in which KM as media object now permeates society. Such as procedure has the goal of opening up and enunciating the ways in which KM as media object now works and affects us, and simultaneously creating the conditions whereby the group dynamics of the occupy movement may function. These tactics will also help to deal with the semiotic flux of capitalism that impinges upon consciousness and forms conditioned responses to objects such as KM. One could argue that the occupy movement is a moment of unconditioning in the continuing fight to stave off the ultimate victory of integrated world capitalism and all that this system signifies.

Conclusion

This chapter has constructed the plateau of April the 29th, 2011, the day of the royal wedding. Since that time, the power of KM as media object has intensified and even undergone a scandal regarding photographs of a topless Kate in the south of France. This scandal kept KM as media object in the news around the world for a period, until the story was replaced by another in the endless media cycle. Now Kate has delivered her first child, and the media are waiting for shots of a postpartum Kate, which I am sure that she is being meticulously groomed and prepared for.

This chapter has theorised the relationships between these quite personal and physical effects of pregnancy, to the impersonal world functioning of capitalism and the overall plane of a capitalised education. The thought of this inter-connectivity is staggering, the scope and range of the possible factors involved in its analysis is virtually unthinkable. However, the immanent materialism of this book gives us one an avenue of exploration and enunciation with respect to bridging the gaps between the reality of KM as media object, knowledge economies and the fluctuations in world trade. Edward Lorenz coined the term 'butterfly effect' which theorised that a hurricane could be contingent on whether or not a butterfly had flapped its wings several weeks earlier. In a more concrete fashion, vast swathes of commercial activity, political opinion and behaviours are now dependent on the actions of one woman, Kate Middleton (KM). Whilst one would not want to add subjective pressure to Kate's current role in Windsor Inc., one can't help but wonder if she can uphold the expectations that have been placed upon her. In a very real, human way, she must overcome the hopes and dreams of a generation in order to try and live and create her own existence (if that's what she wants) and to go beyond the very tenets of KM, a capitalised education, that are continually being recreated in contemporary life.

Conclusion to 'Capitalised Education':

An immanent materialist account of Kate Middleton

What have we learnt from the seven plateaux and what does this book tell us about KM as media object and a capitalised education? Firstly, the plateaux connect in a non-linear fashion, which means that they should be complementary to multiple reading habits. In practice, this means that one can start anywhere in the book and read in different directions before coming to conclusions. Understanding about KM as media object and a capitalised education happens in this manner, with connections between plateaux to be made through multiple readings and thought. Furthermore, these questions figure a reflexive and ongoing project that enables similar studies that connect all elements of this writing, including educational and political analysis, but with a different focus. For example, if the object of a different immanent material study is a celebrity or a politician, the groundings and foundations to the study will alter and this alteration will incur a whole new host of alternating facts and factors with varying degrees of influence. However, the broad factors and lessons that have been learnt from this book remain in place, especially with respect to the matrix around capitalism that the analysis has pointed towards. KM as media object, with the historical and royal precedence of the plateaux, masks a convergent situation where integrated world capitalism and environmental catastrophe are on a broadly collisional course.

One may ask the question: Is there a solution to this convergence of economic crisis and environmental catastrophe in the present day? Certainly, one might cogently look to education and the means of teaching, experimenting with, exploring and learning about an environmentally/politically/socially connected world for the future[109]. We live in one world, on one Earth and in one environment. If the systems that make up this complex yet fragile inter-connected reality are disrupted negatively to such an extent that they are henceforth unable to support human life, the human race will face extinction. This is why the story of KM as media object and a capitalised education are so important. Not to 'save' the human race, as this would re-introduce an unwanted humanism that could morally cloud the arguments, and would act as an intentional barrier to the point of writing about 'capitalised education' in the first place. The point of this book is to express the complex production of KM as media object and a capitalised education, and how this production has personified the ways in which history, events, time and space, desire, becoming and thought have been manipulated and (re)presented to obscure the truth of what was happening (such as the convergence of economics and environmental disaster). As I watched the Royal Flotilla of 2012 on my placid flat-screen television in Australia with growing alarm, I considered all these factors and wondered where the revolution would come from amidst the inane but widespread pomp and ceremony, seemingly taken from a postcard of London in the seventeenth century. KM was there, waving to the crowd, amidst her new family and the servants, dressed in the latest high street trend (or so they hoped) smiling to everyone. I noticed that a few hundred republican, anti-monarchists were herded and controlled in a safe position near to one of the Thames bridges. The flashy, middle to upper class television presenters uniformly berated the protesters for their lack of patriotism. The weather was atrocious, but the spectacle proceeded as planned nonetheless. I thought about the quote from William Burroughs at the start of the introduction to this book, and the smug over-confidence of the whole televised event. I thought: surely the people would eventually rise up and see through this charade as a colossal waste of time, and even worse, as a vulgar and disgusting show of power. But no, everyone involved seemed to be going along with it: "the atmosphere is positively Victorian", one commentator remarked in a jocular fashion directly to the camera, as was mentioned in chapter 3.

The Royal Flotilla of 2012 has made the writing of this book imperative, as I can now see the fundamental problem of KM as media object. This problem is that the herd-like, unthinking and blind behaviours of the past are augmented and exaggerated in the global-media-capitalist-present. Certainly, I am not the only one to point this out. There have been many critical, social and educational thinkers who share my concerns in terms of wanting to give people insight into the power-based manipulations of the existing capitalist elite[110]. The difference that I want to open up through this writing is in terms of the application of immanent materialism to KM as media object is to provide a means to revolutionise political valency. The understanding of and resistance to the ways that KM as media object affects our everyday lives, should not be restricted to alternatives for governance and organisation, for example, that are encapsulated by communism, socialism or in the establishment of a republic. Rather, the use of immanent materialism introduces a form of nomadic politics, which has been much discussed in Deleuzian and feminist literature[111]. Such a politics does not rule out rational responses and alternatives to irrational free-market neoliberalism, wherein KM as a media object has found an appreciative and effective home. Nomadic politics is not idealistic or dualistic in terms of positing one coherent or transcendental field of opposition and resistance to contemporary capitalism. Rather, the politics of this book requires stealth ability, ambush tactics and the silence of the nomad and the skills to be able to blend into social/cultural/intellectual environments if necessary. I would include being a university researcher, lecturer or teacher in with these environments, as these are places where nomadic politics can be taught and learnt. This writing is an example of nomadic politics, in that it does not suggest one unified or unifying subjectivity, which will always work an any situation and in terms of resistance and as a solution to current environmental and economic impasses. Rather, the lessons that this book extols are those of inter-relatedness, expression and serious articulation of the ways in which KM as media object defines a certain historical plateau, and how this convergence of ideas allows imaginative and critical thought around and about this 'power-based' crux. I want a participatory revolution to happen, and I want it to be sustained, penetrating and permanent. As such, I do not want any future revolution that immanent materialism engenders to be shut down or taken over by neoliberal free market 'yeah-sayers', even before it has occurred. I believe this would happen if we are intellectually lazy, or if we allow ourselves to be contained by the systems and modes of thought that are merely in vogue or have emanated from the past. Immanent materialism is a deliberate conceptual and philosophical framework and strategy that allows us not to be misinterpreted or taken up in neoliberal terms, but to plan and execute a revolution in the gaps and in-between of the current global capitalist system.

As such, immanent materialism requires a form of irreverent, reflexive, diffractive, punk philosophy. The analysis of KM as media object incorporates removing many of the 'hooks' of idealism associated with the British royal family and their grip on power through history. To disassociate oneself from these hooks in the analysis is no easy matter, as they have various means to become embedded in thought as right-wing ideology, rigidity and as the triggers that define reactivity against the idea of the royals and the hierarchy that their immovability implies. The royals and their supporters want to present themselves as immovable objects, normalised, justified without recourse to questioning or indexing against other means to organise society. Of course, there are other means to organise, whether it be within in a republic, through a communist state or in a socialist democracy as we are presently seeing in several countries of South America. The point of using immanent materialism for the analysis in contrast to, for example, dialectical materialism, is that one does not posit a singular process through this analysis, whereby the irrationality of the power-based injustices of the past, whether they are capitalist, religious or those of sovereignty, give way to a better and more just society. Žižek[112], for example, would strongly disagree with such an approach, as he argues in, *Less than Nothing*, which is a passionate defence of his use of Hegel and Lacan, and includes a section where he argues against Deleuzian philosophy, especially with respect to the notion of desire that underpins immanent materialism and the ways in which, in his opinion, Deleuze misunderstood the workings of the dialectic. Deleuze's theory of desire in *1000 Plateaus* relies on a flexible, multi-directional plane, whereby desire can move around, and not get caught up irrevocably with one object (such as KM), or with one homogenised mode of becoming. In effect, Deleuze does not counter neoliberal subjectivity with that of the socialist, revolutionary communist or anarchist as oppositional, but deliberately leaves open the type of subjectivity that one takes away from reading the study, in the case of this book about KM and capitalised education, so that one may decide upon action after the processes of synthesis, analysis and under-standing. The Deleuzian political strategy does not reproduce neoliberalism *per se*, the subjectivity associated with the neoliberal state, or the *laissez-faire* rule of the market that favours the capitalised position, but encourages a form of 'transver-salism' or communication between different aspects of subjec-tivity as a mode of differential change and analysis. As Deleuze and Guattari state at the beginning of *1000 Plateaus* about their dual writing practice, "[S]ince each of us was several, there was already quite a crowd,"[113].

In contrast to Žižek, who advocates a form of revolutionary politics based on Hegel, Lacan and Lenin, the Deleuzian plan of action for the self, enacted here through the philosophy of immanent materialism, and described by some as nomadism[114], does not seek contradiction as primary when understanding the current state of affairs. Contrariwise, immanent materialism examines the coincidences, holes and ruptures in the material flows of things in society, and comes to conclusions as series and conjoined conceptual frames, in the case of this study: [KM as media object-capitalised education-x power], where x=a bio-knot of social/political and cultural pulses. What you do with this synthesis and analysis is up to you, not in an individualised or power-based manner, which could be read as taking responsi-bility for actions in the light of the neoliberal agenda, and that positions subjectivity in terms of being rights-based, or as part of proto-civilising society, living a rule-governed existence[115]. Rather, the subjectivity that emerges from the analysis of immanent materialism could be characterised as possessing a probe-head, or node of experimentalism as an interjecting, machinic third term, which relentlessly interrupts the ways in which material complexes define, limit and expand one's sense of power[116]. One could object that such a schema does not allow for a coherent picture of capitalism, or a frame of analysis which would help the reader to understand the point of the synthesis in terms of social critique. Notwithstanding this point about cohesion and framing, a thoroughgoing notion of contemporary capitalism may be built up through the chapters of this book, and by understanding how KM as media object and a capitalised education have come about through a weird, non-linear history. One could perhaps criticise Deleuze and Guattari's semiotically based, schizo-capitalism, as being out of date, as it was conceived and executed in the 1970s, and this characterisation of schizo-capitalism is therefore redundant in today's climate of instanta-neous, global information processing and international capital exchange. However, what isn't out of date is the deployment of the method of immanent materialism in order to come to a new understanding of the ways in which capitalism now works and has changed since the 1970s. Deleuze and Guattari were writing

1000 Plateaus forty years ago, their model of capitalism was deliberately non-static and was consciously designed to be open to novel reworking. One may derive a later and more contemporary model of capitalism and how it continues to work from the 'staggered analysis' of this book, and as eventually focused upon in the plateau of April 29th, 2011, or as: [KM as media object-capitalised education-x power].

In corollary, the chapters of the book have not painted a straightforward or 'additive' picture of the production of KM as media object and a capitalised education. Rather, the production processes that are described here happen in the unconscious as different speeds, lines, flickers of light seen on the periphery of vision, or as odd hallucinations and spheres of unanticipated interest. One should be suspicious of the latest in social theory that looks to explain the whole, or that tries to round up the ways in which we are conditioned and produced in easy to follow 'sound-bites'. Perhaps such work is merely reproducing the ways in which we are currently herded and controlled through media influence, learning theory and global neoliberal domination. Contrariwise, this book looks to make a difference in terms of the production of KM as media object and a capitalised education by drawing a lateral plane whereby connections between the production of KM as media object, capitalised education and political-social and cultural power may become apparent. This lateral plane happens in words and through imaginative conceptual construction, and should have 'real world' consequences in terms of the ways in which we gather, socialise and speak. The most conspicuous consequence of such an analysis is to come to a new way to talk about KM as media object and learning, one that is relieved of the power-related webs that have come to cluster around KM, specifically to sell commercial products and to substantiate and ferment an attitude to the world that upholds the (re)creation of the British royal family in the present mode of capitalism, however one might reconcile this mode and its changing nature. However, immanent materialism is not a type of discourse analysis, nor a straightforward counter theory to the maintenance of the status quo. The crude inequalities that are demonstrated and have been augmented via the production of KM as media object and her capitalised education are not magically resolved though immanent materialism. Rather, immanence works in the gaps and ruptures that are currently playing out through KM, and through specific material, social and cultural flows that may be attended to with Heraclitean resolve. As Nick Srnicek has stated with respect to assemblage theory:

> The proliferation of identities and collective movements, the tendency towards non-state movements (whether at a global or local level), and the Western world's recognition of Otherness and alterity have, in turn, made any notion of a homogeneous people impossible to sustain. The result of all these tendencies has been to produce an increasingly complex and dynamic world – one to which political science is still trying to acclimate.[117]

Notes

Introduction

1. William S. Burroughs, *The Western Lands* (London: Picador, 1987), p. 137.

2. See, for example, David Bissell, "Comfortable bodies: sedentary affects," *Environment and Planning 40* (2008): 1697-1712.

3. Gregory Bateson, *Steps to an Ecology of Mind* (New York: Ballantine Books, 1972) p. 113.

4. Please do not misunderstand the point here. I am fascinated by the uncontrolled proliferation of non-specialist thinkers in the field. I do, however, retain the point that a philosophical position must be constructed through deep reflective practice, widespread usage, and henceforth maintained across relevant fields to have political valency. I believe that immanent materialism has the capacity to do all of these tasks.

5. The *umwelt* is the perceptual position in which organisms exist. Jakob von Uexküll studied organisms such as ticks, jellyfish and sea urchins, and developed a theory of their worlds as subjects; i.e. fully embedded in bio-semiological systems that explain how they experience the world. As such, complex 'life' is ascribed to the most basic of organisms.

6. McKenzie Wark, *Virtual Geography: Living with Global Media Events* (Bloomington and Indianapolis: Indiana University Press, 1994).

7. See, David R Cole, *Traffic jams: Analysing everyday life through the Immanent Materialism of Deleuze and Guattari* (New York: Punctum Books, 2013).

8. Christian Kerslake, "Deleuze and the Meanings of Immanence", Paper for 'After 68', Jan van Eyck Academy, Maastricht, 16th June, 2009, p. 35.

Chapter I

9. See, David R Cole, "Education and the Politics of Cyberpunk", *Review of Education, Pedagogy and Cultural Studies*, 27 (2) (2005) 159-170.

10. Jean Baudrillard, *Symbolic Exchange and Death*, trans. Iain Hamilton Grant (London: Sage Publications, 1993). This is a pivotal text with respect to understanding this point with respect to the foundations of consumerism.

11. See, for example, Chris Hables Gray, ed., *The Cyborg Handbook* (London: Routledge, 1995)

12. See, David R Cole, "Virtual Terrorism and the Internet E-Learning Options", *E-Learning*, 4 (2) (2007) 116-127.

13. Gilles Deleuze and Félix Guattari, *Anti-Oedipus and 1000 Plateaus: Capitalism and Schizophrenia I and II* (London: The Athlone Press, 1984 and 1988).

14. See, Slavoj Žižek, *Organs Without Bodies: Deleuze and Consequences* (New York: Routledge, 2004)

15. See, Benjamin Noys, *The Persistence of the Negative: A Critique of Contemporary Continental Theory*, (Edinburgh: Edinburgh UP, 2010) for an interesting discussion of capitalism and the negativity of thought in relation to continental philosophy.

16. A fascinating read with respect to this point about nihilism is, Ray Brassier, *Nihil Unbound: Enlightenment and Extinction* (Houndmills: Palgrave Macmillan, 2007).

17. Eugene Thacker, *In the Dust of this Planet: Horror of Philosophy, vol. 1* (Winchester: Zero Books, 2010).

18. See, David R Cole, "Techno-shamanism and Educational Research", *Ashe! Journal of Experimental Spirituality*, Rebel Satori Press, Hulls Cove, ME, 6, (2007) 1-32.

19. These subject-object relations in social theory are an important part of *1000 Plateaus*. For a critique of this position see, Ray Brassier, "Concepts and Objects", in Levi Bryant, Nick Srnicek and Graham Harman, eds., *The*

Speculative Turn: Continental Materialism and Realism (Prahan, Victoria: re.press, 2011) pp. 47-66.

20. See, Glenn Rikowski, "Value—The Life Blood of Capitalism: Knowledge is the Current Key", *Policy Futures in Education*, 1 (1) (2003) 160-178.

21. See, for example: http://www.rav.net.au/assets/street-theatre-essentials-teacher-notes.pdf for an example of such a unit of work.

22. See: http://www.youtube.com/watch?v=7VUy-wBwBvw

23. See, for example, Diana Masny and David R Cole, *Multiple Literacies Theory: A Deleuzian Perspective* (Rotterdam: Sense Publications).

24. Mark Fisher, *Capitalist Realism* (Winchester: Zero Books, 2009).

Chapter 2

25. Go to: http://www.bbc.co.uk/archive/ww2outbreak/7918.sh tml to listen to the speech.

26. See, Gilles Deleuze, *Essays Critical and Clinical*, trans. Daniel W. Smith and Michael A. Grego (London: Verso, 1998), pp. 107-115.

27. See: http://www.vintageadbrowser.com/tobacco-ads-1930s for some excellent examples of healthy smoking advertising.

28. See, for example, information regarding the relationship between lung cancer and smoking at: http://en.wiki pedia.org/wiki/Lung_cancer

29. See, M.J. Jappy, *Danger UXB: The Remarkable Story of the Disposal of Unexploded Bombs During the Second World War* (London: Channel 4 books, 2001).

30. See, for example, David R Cole, ed., *Surviving Economic Crises through Education* (New York: Peter Lang, 2012).

31. See, for example, The Invisible Committee, *The Coming Insurrection* (Cambridge, Mass.: Semiotext(e), 2009). In this book, the committee give a credible analysis of work and

non-work and their social effects and attitudes.

32. Donna Haraway, "The Promises of Monsters: A Regenerative Politics for Inappropriate/d Others". In L. Grossberg, C. Nelson and P. A. Treichler, (Eds.), *Cultural Studies* (pp. 295-337) (New York: Routledge, 1992) p. 231.

33. Umberto Eco, "Casablanca, or, The Clichés are Having a Ball". In Sonia Maasik and Jack Solomon, eds., *Signs of Life in the USA: Readings on Popular Culture* (Boston: Bedford Books, 1994) pp. 260-264.

34. See, John Calder, ed., *A William Burroughs Reader* (Bungay: Pan Books, 1982).

35. See, Gilles Deleuze, *Cinema I: The Movement-Image and Cinema II: The Time-Image*, trans. Hugh Tomlinson and Barbara Habberjam, Hugh Tomlinson and Robert Galeta (London: The Athlone Press, 1992 and London: Continuum, 2005).

Chapter 3

36. See, for example, *G. E. Moore: Selected Writings*, T. Baldwin (ed.), (Routledge: London, 1993).

37. An archive of Thomas Hill Green's work can be found at: http://archive.org/search.php?query=thomas%20hill%20gre en

38. See, G. W. F. Hegel, *Phenomenology of Spirit*, trans. A. V. Miller. (Oxford: Oxford University Press, 1977). [originally published 1807]

39. Karl Marx, *Capital Vol. 3, in: Marx/Engels Collected Works* (London, International Publishers, 1976) p. 50.

40. See Jason Read, *The Micro-Politics of Capital: Marx and the Prehistory of the Present* (New York: Albany NY Press, 2003).

41. See: http://mailstar.net/rhodes-will.html for further explanation of Cecil Rhodes' writings.

42. K. Marx, *A Contribution to the Critique of Political Economy* (Moscow: Progress Publishers, 1977). Online at: http://www

.marxists.org/archive/marx/works/1859/critique-pol-economy/preface.htm

43. Philip José Farmer, "Farmer on Wilson" an essay on Robert Anton Wilson in *Heavy Metal* #54 (September 1981).

44. Aleister Crowley, *Magick: Book Four, Liber Aba* (York Beach, Maine: Saule Weiser, Inc., 1994).

45. "A Venerable Orang-outang", a caricature from the March 22, 1871 issue of *The Hornet* magazine.

46. Benjamin Disraeli, *Sybil; or The Two Nations* (Oxford: Oxford University, 1844) p. 145.

47. Karl Marx, *The Economic and Philosophic Manuscripts of 1844.* Online at: https://www.marxists.org/archive/marx/works/1844/manuscripts/labour.htm

48. George Bernard Shaw, *Pygmalion* (New York: Bartleby Com, 1999) [original play published 1916].

49. Karl Marx and Frederick Engels, *The Communist Manifesto.* Available as an e-Book at: http://manybooks.net/titles/marxengelsetext93manif12.html

Chapter 4

50. See, for example, David R Cole, "The mediation of teacher education", *AARE 2004 International Education Research Conference Paper Abstracts*, Melbourne, Australia, EJ (2004).

51. Sadi Carnot, *Reflections on the Motive Power of Heat and on Machines Fitted to Develop That Power*, trans. Robert Henry Thurston (New York: J. Wiley and Sons, 1890). [original French text 1824]

52. See, David K. Hulse, *The early development of the steam engine* (Leamington Spa: TEE Publishing, 1999).

53. See, for example, P. Crutzen and C. Schwargel, "Living in the Anthropocene: Towards a New Global Ethos", *Environment 360* January 2011. Available at: http://e360.yale.edu/feature/living_in_the_anthropocene_toward_a_new_global_ethos/2363/

54. See, Kirkpatrick Sale, *Rebels against the Future: the Luddites and their war on the Industrial Revolution: lessons for the computer age* (New York: Perseus Books, 1995).

55. Auguste Comte, *A General View of Positivism*, trans. J.H. Bridges (London: Trübner and Co, 1856).

56. Iain Hamilton Grant, *Philosophies of Nature after Schelling* (London: Bloomsbury, 2008).

57. See, D. Coole, and S. Frost, eds., *New Materialisms: Ontology, Agency, and Politics* (Durham: Duke University Press, 2010).

58. Joseph Lawrence, "Philosophical Religion and the Quest for Authenticity," In Jason Wirth, ed., *Schelling Now: Contemporary Readings* (Bloomington: Indiana University Press, 2005) p. 16.

59. David R Cole, *Educational Life Forms: Deleuzian Teaching and Learning Practice* (Rotterdam: Sense Publishers, 2011).

60. See, David R Cole, "Affective Literacies: Deleuze, Discipline and Power", in Inna Semetsky and Diana Masny, eds., *Deleuze and Education* (Edinburgh: Edinburgh University Press, 2013) pp. 94-112.

61. See, Gilles Deleuze, *Bergsonism*, trans. Hugh Tomlinson and Barbara Habberjam (New York: Zone Books, 1991).

62. For example, J. Stiglitz, *Globalisation and its discontents* (London: Penguin Books, 2002).

63. Go to: http://schwartztronica.wordpress.com/2012/05/22/capitalist-realism-homo-capitalus-homo-financus/

64. See, Philip Goodchild, "Philosophy as a Way of Life: Deleuze on Thinking and Money", *SubStance*, Volume 39, Number 1, 2010 (issue 121).

65. Edward Said, *Orientalism* (London: Penguins Books, 1977).

66. George Orwell, *The Road to Wigan Pier* (Harmondsworth: Penguin Books, 1988).

67. Inga Clendinnen, Boyer Lectures, "Inside the Contact Zone: Part 1", 5 December 1999.

Chapter 5

68. See, Patrick King, "Deleuze, Guattari, and Lenin: The Uses of Time and History for Revolutionary Politics". Available online at: http://canononline.org/archives/current-issue/deleuze-guattari-and-lenin-the-uses-of-time-and-history-for-revolutionary-politics/

69. See, for example, Slavoj Žižek, "Can Lenin tell us about freedom today?" Available online at: http://www.lacan.com/freedom.htm

70. For further explanation of this point see, for example, Éric Alliez and Andrew Goffey, eds., *The Guattari Effect* (London: Continuum, 2011).

71. For example, Lev Vygotsky, *Thought and Language* (Cambridge, MA.: MIT Press, 1962).

72. See, for example, R. van de Veer and J. Valsiner, eds., *The Vygotsky Reader* (Oxford: Blackwell, 1994). There are many nuanced sides of the debate around Vygotsky's writings and their (mis)translations into English that could be mentioned at this point. René van der Veer's opinions are authoritative in this area.

73. However, one could argue that Nietzsche is perhaps one of the least fascist writers and philosophers who has ever lived. Nazi ideology was an utter distortion and reinvention of Nietzsche.

74. Gilles Deleuze and Félix Guattari, *1000 Plateaus: Capitalism and Schizophrenia II*, trans. Brian Massumi (London: The Athlone Press, 1988) p. 230.

75. Speeches by Reich Chancellor Adolf Hitler the Leader of the New Germany. With an introduction by Dr. Joseph Goebbels. Berlin: Liebheit and Thiesen, 1933. Find at: http://archive.org/details/TheNewGermanyDesiresWorkAndPeace

76. #Accelerate: Manifesto for an accelerationist politics. Article 24 (Williams and Srnicek). There has been a recent special

edition of e-flux on accelerationism: http://www.e-flux. com/issues/46-june-2013/

77. See David R Cole, "Lost in Data Space: Using Nomadic Analysis to Perform Social Science", in Rebecca Coleman and Jessica Ringrose, eds., *Deleuze and Research Methodologies* (Edinburgh: Edinburgh University Press, 2013) pp. 219-238.

78. Eugene Holland, *Nomadic Citizenship: free-market communism and the slow-motion strike* (Minneapolis: University of Minnesota Press, 2011) p. 29.

79. See also, Jane Bennett, *Vibrant Matter: A Political Ecology of Things* (Durham: Duke University Press, 2010).

Chapter 6

80. King Henry II, son of Count Geoffrey Plantagenet of Anjou and the Empress Matilda, daughter of King Henry I of England and widow of Emperor Henry V, assumes the throne of England after a generation of civil war (1137-1153) between his uncle King Stephen of Blois and his mother. By inheritance, Henry II was 1) King of England, 2) Duke of Normandy, 3) Count of Anjou. (Together Henry II's holdings are called "The Angevin Empire").

81. See, for example, Christopher Harper-Bill and Nicholas Vincent, eds., *Henry II: New Interpretations.* (Woodbridge, UK: Boydell Press, 2007).

82. Giorgio Agamben, *State of Exception*, trans. Kevin Attell (Chicago: The University of Chicago Press, 2005).

83. This point is in addition to the use of 'the Crown' as metonymy.

84. Andrea Capellanus, *The Art of Courtly Love*, trans. John Jay Parry (New York: Columbia University Press, 1941).

85. Geoffrey of Monmouth, *The History of the Kings of Britain*, trans. Lewis Thorpe (London: Penguin Books, 1966).

86. *One Thousand Plateaus*, pp. 149-167.

87. Georges Bataille, *Eroticism*, trans. Mary Dalwood (London: Marion Boyars, 1987). Stendhal, *Love*, trans. Gilbert and Suzanne Sale (Harmondsworth: Penguin Classics, 1975).

88. Giorgio Agamben, *What is an Apparatus? And other essays*, trans. David Kishik and Stefan Pedatella (Stanford: Stanford University Press, 2009).

89. See, for example, Liz Stanley and Sue Wise, *Breaking Out Again: Feminist Ontology and Epistemology* (New Edition) (London: Routledge, 1993).

90. See, David R Cole, "The Reproduction of Philosophical Bodies in Education with Language", *Educational Philosophy and Theory*, Volume 42, Number 8, December 816-829 (2010).

91. Gilles Deleuze and Félix Guattari, *1000 Plateaus: Capitalism and Schizophrenia II*, trans. Brian Massumi (London: The Athlone Press, 1988) pp. 387-468.

92. Ibid. p. 392.

Chapter 7

93. See, for example, L. Suarez-Villa, *Technocapitalism: A Critical Perspective on Technological Innovation and Corporatism* (Philadelphia: Temple University Press, 2009).

94. See, David Farrell Krell, ed., *Martin Heidegger: Basic Writings* (London, Routledge, 1993).

95. Gilles Deleuze, *Difference and Repetition*, trans. Paul Patton (London: The Athlone Press, 1994) p. 32.

96. See, for example, Mark Olssen, "Understanding the mechanisms of neoliberal control: lifelong learning, flexibility and knowledge capitalism," in Andreas Fejes and Katherine Nicoll, eds., *Foucault and Lifelong Learning: Governing the subject*, (London and New York: Routledge, 2008) pp. 34 – 47.

97. *Difference and Repetition*. p. 192.

98. Gilbert Simondon, L'individu et sa genèse physio-biologique (Paris: PUF, 1964).

99. See, for example, T. Terranova, *Network Culture: Politics for*

the Information Age (London: Pluto, 2004).

100. Christian Marazzi, *The Violence of Financial Capitalism*, trans. Kristina Lebedeva and Jason Francis McGimsey (New York: Semiotext(e), 2010). Maurizio Lazzarato, *The Making of the Indebted Man*, trans. Joshua David Jordan (New York: Semiotext(e), 2012).

101. See, for example, David Harvey, *The Enigma of Capital: And the Crises of Capitalism* (London: Oxford University press, 2010).

102. Stephen S. Ball, *Global Education Inc.: New Policy Networks and the Neoliberal Imaginary* (London: Routledge, 2012) and, *Education Plc: Understanding private sector participation in public sector education.* (London and New York: Routledge, 2007).

103. François Laruelle, "The Decline of Materialism in the Name of Matter", *Pli: The Warwick Journal of Philosophy* 12 (2001) p. 34.

104. See, David R Cole, "Matter in Motion: The Educational Materialism of Gilles Deleuze", *Educational Philosophy and Theory*, Volume 44, Number S1, May, 3-17 (2012).

105. See, for example, Arkady Plotnitsky, *Complementarity: Anti-Epistemology after Bohr and Derrida* (Durham and London: Duke University Press, 1994).

106. Marco Deseriis and Jodi Dean, "A Movement Without Demands?" *Possible Futures*, a project of the Social Science Research Council. Available at: http://www.thething.it/snafu/?p=726

107. See, Franco Beradi, *Finance and Poetry* (New York: Semiotext(e), 2012).

108. See, Félix Guattari, *Chaosmosis: An Ethico-Aesthetic Paradigm*, trans. P. Bains and J. Pefanis (Bloomington: Indiana University Press, 1995).

Conclusion

109. See, David R Cole, ed., *Surviving Economic Crises through Education* (New York: Peter Lang, 2012)

110. For example, Scott Lash and Celia Lury, *Global Culture Industry: The Mediation of Things* (Cambridge: Polity Press, 2007).

111. For example, Rosie Braidotti's, *Nomadic Subjects* (New York: Columbia University Press, 1994) and Eugene Holland, *Nomadic Citizenship: free-market communism and the slow-motion strike* (Minneapolis: University of Minnesota Press, 2011).

112. Slavoj Žižek, *Less than Zero: Hegel and the Shadow of Dialectical Materialism* (London: Verso, 2012).

113. Gilles Deleuze and Felix Guattari, *1000 Plateaus: Capitalism and Schizophrenia II* (London: The Athlone Press, 1988), p. 3.

114. For example, Hakim Bey, *T. A. Z. The Temporary Autonomous Zone, Ontological Anarchy, Poetic Terrorism* (Brooklyn, NY: Autonomedia, 1991) and, Jean-François Lyotard, *Driftworks*, ed., Roger McKeon (New York: Semiotext(e), 1984) [Essays and interviews dating from 1970-72].

115. For example, John Rawls, *A Theory of Justice* (Cambridge, MA: Harvard University Press, 1971).

116. See, David R Cole, "Virtual Terrorism and the Internet E-Learning Options", *E-Learning*, 4 (2) (2007) 116-127.

117. Nick Srnicek, "Assemblage Theory, Complexity and Contentious Politics: The Political Ontology of Gilles Deleuze", Unpublished Ph.D. thesis, London School of Economics, 2013.

Contemporary culture has eliminated both the concept of the public and the figure of the intellectual. Former public spaces – both physical and cultural – are now either derelict or colonized by advertising. A cretinous anti-intellectualism presides, cheerled by expensively educated hacks in the pay of multinational corporations who reassure their bored readers that there is no need to rouse themselves from their interpassive stupor. The informal censorship internalized and propagated by the cultural workers of late capitalism generates a banal conformity that the propaganda chiefs of Stalinism could only ever have dreamt of imposing. Zer0 Books knows that another kind of discourse – intellectual without being academic, popular without being populist – is not only possible: it is already flourishing, in the regions beyond the striplit malls of so-called mass media and the neurotically bureaucratic halls of the academy. Zer0 is committed to the idea of publishing as a making public of the intellectual. It is convinced that in the unthinking, blandly consensual culture in which we live, critical and engaged theoretical reflection is more important than ever before.